THE SEARCH FOR GOD

By the same author

THE COMING OF THE THIRD CHURCH
An analysis of the present and future of the Church

COURAGE, CHURCH!
Essays in Ecclesial Spirituality

THE MISSIONS ON TRIAL
A moral for the future from the archives of today

142871

BR
127
.B7613
1980

Walbert Bühlmann

THE SEARCH
FOR GOD

**An encounter with the peoples
and religions of Asia**

ORBIS BOOKS

Maryknoll, New York 10545

GOSHEN COLLEGE LIBRARY
GOSHEN, INDIANA

The Catholic Foreign Mission Society of America (Maryknoll) recruits and trains people for overseas missionary service. Through Orbis Books Maryknoll aims to foster the international dialogue that is essential to mission. The books published, however, reflect the opinions of their authors and are not meant to represent the official position of the society.

Translated from the German by B. Krokosz, assisted by A. P. Dolan

Copyright © Walbert Bühlmann
English translation copyright © St Paul Publications 1979

U.S. edition 1980 by Orbis Books, Maryknoll, NY 10545

All rights reserved

Typeset in Great Britain and printed and bound in The United States of America

Library of Congress Cataloging in Publication Data

Bühlmann, Walbert.
  The search for God.

  Translation of Alle haben denselben Gott.
  Bibliography: p.
  1. Christianity and other religions.
2. Religions. I. Title.
BR127.B7613   1980   261.2   80-15732
ISBN 0-88344-450-X (pbk.)

Contents

5

Foreword

ONE can never quite penetrate the mystery of religions, just as one cannot totally comprehend the notion of conscience. Both are realities which are experienced daily, but which somehow cannot be apprehended. Today they are precisely a mystery reaching far out beyond the individual, an inclination, a nostalgia striving for new horizons which really turn people into individuals, into a person who is more than just a dissectible mass of flesh with a mind that can be analysed, a being, who in all his enjoyment, economic progress and scientific achievements can never wholly explain his actions.

In the past, the Church was primarily concerned with individuals by preaching morality and asceticism to them in order to sanctify them and to save their souls. It granted spiritual and individualistic salvation. Today, now that it is faced with more important tasks, the Church has to expand its boundaries. It is a question of life and death, perhaps even a question of a new hope, in the discussion with Marxism, secularism and in the fascinating undertaking of the coming together of the religions.

There are different ways of approaching the Asian religions. One could, as an outsider, and without really knowing much about them, examine them and then state the verdict. This was the approach in previous centuries and was the traditional "solution" to the problem. People took their places in divided camps and tried to overcome, eradicate, or at best, bring the enemy to their knees by

7

baptism.[2] One could study them a little more closely in order to discover their positive values and to make them public. This is the theological approach, which, for centuries has produced a lot of research, but in addition, has confused many Christians.[3] Finally one could try to build a bridge between one school of thought to the other and pave the way for a mutual exchange of ideas. This is the new, pastoral approach, which either points out theoretically what could and should happen, or shows factually what is hapening at present. The latter, pragmatic approach is the one we shall take.

Around 1960 Professor Thomas Ohm published a study which caused quite a stir at the time. It was called *Asia's "No" and "Yes" to Western Christianity*. It was a critical analysis of many Asian voices of opinion towards Christianity; indeed, it was chiefly a polemic and apologetic piece of work, in as far as it signified the end of one epoch and at the same time denoted the beginning of a new era. I should now like to bring this book up to date, to relate what has happened during the 20 years since its publication. On the basis of the numerous interreligious conferences and meetings — a typical phenomenon of this new era — I should like to portray how, gradually, progress was made towards a dialogue which somehow did not quite materialise into perfection, how people bit by bit worked up towards a world shrine of religions, and yet did not feel completely at home in it. However, by searching even further and building up even more, one will increasingly discover not the identity of Christianity, but rather how it is a complement to the other religions, and this in itself brings joy to the heart.

Why, then, not make a report of a journey and follow the trails of this special mystery of religions? Since 1961 the author has six times spent a short or long period of time in altogether 12 countries between the Middle and Far East. He was not a member of the above mentioned conferences, but he knows the localities where they took place; he studied the published conference reports and spoke to experts who took part. In this way he took poetic licence to present the conferences in the form of a reporter's account, in order to give a lively impression to the exciting content.

This book is in no way aimed simply at Asia or those interested in Asia. If perchance fate allows the Asian religions to meet together with Christianity on intimate terms, then it also applies conversely to Christianity. In such an encounter both partners are winners. Whoever lives in the mystery of religion himself will be glad of the extension of the religious horizons.

Fr Walbert Bühlmann OFMCap

1

All Roads Lead to Asia

TWO thousand years ago everyone knew that all roads led to Rome. The Roman Empire stood at the peak of its power, and its emperors and cohorts always used to return to Rome after the victorious battles. In the last 500 years one could modify that phrase and say: All roads lead to Europe. Europe had taken over the heritage of the German Reich, it had extended its borders beyond the ocean, and had become the centre and the zenith, the core and the intellectual leader of the world. The threads of world economy, world politics and the world Church were all intertwined here. Every decision for the rest of the world was taken here. All sorts of people were drawn to the major cities of Europe.

Have we already resigned ourselves to this latest and certainly the future version of the phrase that all roads lead to Asia? Since the second World War, in any case, our customary view of life has changed fundamentally. In Africa 50 independent states have come into being, which at present, together with the Near East, are forming the political trouble spots of the world. Since the end of the war in Vietnam Asia seems in fact to have been pushed further back, and for many people it has yet again become the "Far East", separated by enormous distances as well as an impenetrable spirituality. In any case, it is not situated in the centre of their interest. Are these people well informed with their attitudes? Or are they not living 30 years behind the times with the knowledge they possess?

Over the past 30 years things have been happening which have changed our world. China, which had always been called "Empire of the Centre", has in fact actually become the Empire of the Centre. With its population of 800 million it has more inhabitants than Africa and Latin America put together, not to mention its infiltration into the whole of the Third World. Asia as a whole accounts for 56% of the world population. In the year 2000 this figure will probably rise to 60%. With Asia on one side and all the other continents on the other, the scale will tip towards Asia. Faced with this mass of yellow people, should we be talking about the yellow danger, or about the yellow threat, the yellow future, or even the yellow hope? As always, we simply cannot ignore Asia.

Politically and economically the Pacific has taken the rôle of the most important ocean after the Mediterranean and the Atlantic. Four of the six world powers are situated around it: the USA with its increasing emphasis towards the Pacific, the USSR with the rapid development in Siberia, Japan as the world's third economic power, and China with its massive human, economic and ideological potential. Going about it in a logical way, one would have to reform the usual world map with Europe in the centre, that is, by moving the two Americas to the right in order to produce the new centre in the Pacific. The Arabic bloc, half of which belongs to Asia, is also to be taken seriously as a new economic power; Europe, on the other hand, which obviously still ranks highly — especially to the extent that it is becoming a unified Europe — is just managing to survive, as though it were isolated on the edge of a new map of the world, perhaps even in future world history. Truly, whether we like it or not, we have to reckon with Asia. The new roads do lead to Asia.

If the Pacific ocean has become the new centre of the world, it has at the same time presented a line of demarcation between two worlds, namely the christian and the non-christian world. To the east of this ocean lie the two Americas, which are more or less christian continents. Even further to the east are Europe and Africa, again, more or less christian continents, for even black Africa will have a christian majority by the year 2000. In the south Pacific we meet the christian countries of the Philippines, Papua-New Guinea and Australia. In the west, however, lies the colossus of Asia as the pronounced non-christian continent. Of the 2.3 billion Asians, the 52 million Catholics form only 2.27%, to which must be added 11 million Protestants and 3 million Orthodox (not counting Russia). If we disregard the 32 million Catholics from the Philippines, the percentage of Catholics in Asia falls to 0.86% and that of Christians to 1.47%. After four centuries of missionary work we are still virtually at square one!

The seemingly favourable proportion of five christian continents against one non-christian one looks in fact much more tragic, since Asia constitutes the large majority of the world's population. One wonders why it happened that Asia, of all continents, where all the great religions found their inspiration and took their roots — Hinduism, Buddhism, Shintoism, Confucianism, Islam and even Christianity — why has this fate come to such a religious Asia?

This continent is "guilty" by the fact that still two-thirds of the population is non-christian. A few years ago, public opinion stated that the number of Christians between now and the year 2000 will fall from the present 32% to 16%, due mainly to the population explosion in Asia. More reliable calculations, however, have revealed that this is not the case, but that we Christians will most likely not be able to maintain the present proportion.[1] That is certainly one consolation. At the same time we have to resign ourselves to the fact that the pace of our missionary work will never break through the "sound barrier" and that we obviously cannot get through to that other two-thirds.

Why is it, then, that such a religious continent, is, and is continuing to be so little influenced by Christianity? Does the fault lie with those "heathens" who did not want to be

13

converted, or are we Christians to blame for not using the right methods? Or does the answer lie more deeply than that, hidden in the secret of salvation history? Must every person who seeks salvation really be expelled from his community and be incorporated into the Church? Are not these other religions also a way towards salvation? Has the second Vatican Council, which has seen so many things in a new light, not also cast aside certain opinions of paganism? What in fact is the will of God in all the different religions? Should they really be adopted, judged or even eradicated? Is it possible to make a virtue of necessity by the fact that Asia is now non-christian? There are numerous questions which are urgently awaiting new, productive and prophetic answers. We all know that we cannot get anywhere with previous conceptions.

As long as Europe held world supremacy, as long as Christianity, too, was regarded not only because of the faith but also because of its position as a European religion as well as, naturally, the world religion, as long as the pagans lived far away from Europe and presented no serious threat, for centuries one could pass uncontradicted judgements upon them and be left with only one concern: to baptise the people and thereby gloriously spread the Church around the whole world. After seeing that from the start we never succeeded in doing this in Asia during four centuries, and after seeing that those people have become our trading partners, our political fellow sufferers, our friends at universities, embassies, UN centres, in short, our adult comrades with equal rights in the streets and in the same world, one suddenly realises, not without some shame, that previous misconceptions must be done away with and that new interpretations are now due. Above all one realises that in addition to missionary work and conversion to Christianity, it is obvious that yet a further possibility must be offered towards creating a harmonious, human co-existence.

What, then, have the missions already achieved? What are 52 million Catholics compared with 2.3 billion Asians?

From 1972 to 1975 the number of Catholics increased by two million, whilst the population of Asia increased by 154 million. Of those 52 million, a large proportion came from the old, the poor, the caste-less and the sick. The strongholds of the Asian high religions, on the other hand, have not once been shattered by the century-long onslaught of Christianity.

Today the situation is a profoundly different one. We have become a new world politically and economically in the tide of events, a world with transport and mass media. We acknowledge the human rights with "equality of all persons without any discrimination of race, colour, sex, tongue or religion" (Article 2 of the Universal Declaration of Human Rights). Even within the Church, the latest document of the Vatican Council on freedom of religion and of conscience has been accepted, although it first had to overcome a long period of opposition from certain circles. In addition, what the missions have failed to achieve has been successfully carried out by secularisation. This has been done by the break up of these religions from within, so that today, millions of Muslims, Hindus, etc., even Christians, have abandoned their religious beliefs and practices and have lost their former security. They are thereby becoming much more open about religious discussions, no longer in the form of controversy, but as an existentialist question that ponders the ultimate meaning of life.

Today, all this contributes to building a link of utmost historical importance between Christianity and the Asian religions. There is no longer a one-sided attempt at conversion to Christianity; on the contrary, both partners are experiencing something quite new and overwhelming by their mutual efforts at trying to understand each other. After seeing the successful model of Africa as the sensational continent for missionary work over the past 30 years, people in Asia are now engaged in turning over a new leaf and making a fresh start with the unsuccessful history of missionary work — which, after all was so successful that it managed to build up a living Church conducive to dialogue! The emphasis of this new chapter in history is on mutual discovery, recognition and exchange of ideas, and on trying to work towards unity by living and growing together. Did Thomas Ohm not have some insight, at least an idea, that Asia was perhaps to render a similar service to the Church as the Reformation did?[2] A few years ago such a supposition and a comparison of the Reformation would have sounded "shattering to pious hearts" or even slanderous. Nowadays we have learnt to face facts and the realities of life. Geographical exploration and political control of Asia now belong to the past. The future calls for the spiritual investigation of this continent, which is as new, as exciting, as full of risks and promises as the exploration of the universe by the astronauts.

After the exemplary encounter of Christianity with Greek and Roman cultures, and then — already less original — with the Germanic world, there followed centuries of statistics, repetition and exportation of western theology, liturgy and Church discipline to the other continents. Now, through Pope John and his Vatican Council, Christianity seems to have become freed of its old, fixed ideas and with its renewal has become more flexible to take new paths, to make fresh judgements and to adopt new values towards embarking on this confrontation with the Asian religions, which by fate is moving back to the era of the early centuries, with the difference that it is far superior in its quantitative extent and its qualitative individuality. This is the exciting moment of history which we are living here and now. Asia, the one and only non-christian continent, has saved this surprise of Christendom until now.

However, one cannot isolate this new dialogue with the religions from the other dialogue which is equally precarious and auspicious: the dialogue with Marxism. Both these fronts constitute an immense challenge for the Church. It is a question of the two dimensions, the two aspirations of the individual who wants to improve his standard of living and who wants to live forever. The Churches are clearly divided between these two partners in the dialogue; perhaps they have something to learn by all this, perhaps they could receive help which would enable them to serve people in a better way. It is a plausible thought that on the question of the ultimate meaning of life, all religions should work together, so that people are not deceived by secularism in their final hopes. Is it not also a plausible thought, that looking at all the inequality and poverty in the world, the two greatest spiritual forces, the two "messiahs" of history, should hold out their hand to each other and try to accomplish the tremendous task of giving all men equal opportunities and new hopes, instead of fighting each other? Faced with such questions and challenges, our internal problems of the Church will suddenly become only minor problems, which will consequently have to be seen and resolved in conjunction with the problems of the world. To the geographical, demographic and spiritual extent of Asia, we can begin to understand the need for the right proportions.

If, in the political sphere, for example, in the Near East question, against all the obvious conflicting viewpoints, the negotiations do not break down, or are not allowed to be discontinued for the sake of peace in the world, how much more must we leave nothing undone in these two spheres of theological and ideological disagreement, in order to transform this confrontation into coexistence and complementary enrichment? Are all these considerations merely utopian? Perhaps they are. But then one should know that in the past utopian thoughts were always the most powerful forces of inspiration, and only they could ever get the ball rolling again.

2

Thoughts on Heroes of the Past

IN the archives and cemeteries from Port Said to Sydney, and from Singapore to Seoul we can read stories which to us nowadays seem almost like something taken out of a book. It all began with the travels of Marco Polo who, in 1271, at the age of 17, accompanied his father and his uncle on an expedition to Asia. Until his return in 1295 he had been through nearly every country in Asia, travelling even as far as Peking. His accounts on the wonders of the world caused a sensation in the whole of Europe.

At the same time, and often before the well known explorers and travellers, the missionaries also set foot in Asia. These were the Franciscans and the Dominicans in the thirteenth and fourteenth centuries, the Jesuits, the Carmelites and the Capuchins in the sixteenth and seventeenth centuries. These, too, travelled across Persia, India, Tibet and China, and brought us valuable information about those lands and peoples. From the nineteenth century onwards, the activity spread and a host of missionary and sisterhood communities were opened in order to proclaim the gospel to the Asian people. Thousands of these remained permanently in Asia.

When we consider that nowadays it is possible to fly from Europe to Bombay in seven hours, and in a further seven hours to arrive somewhere in the Far East, we can only be amazed how those missionaries covered the huge distances and how they survived the years and the decades.

Let us take a classic example, that of St Francis Xavier. His journey from Lisbon to Goa is described by his critical biographer G. Schurhammer in 130 pages.[3] It reads like a novel, but it is supported wholly by contemporary sources. On April 7, 1541, the flag-ship Santiago, weighing 700 tons, left Portugal in a convoy of five other ships. On each side of the bow hung an 18 cwt anchor as a security in storms and against sandbanks. If one was lucky, one would hope to cover the 3000 miles by sea within six months without going on shore. For such a long time it was necessary to bring drinking water and provisions for the 360 men, especially for the soldiers and sailors and a number of privileged guests.

After only two days Francis Xavier knew what it was like to be sea-sick. This experience lasted two months. Near the equator, in the inferno of Guinea, they met up with the dreaded calm: for 40 days the ships and their passengers lay there motionless in the stifling heat and in the terrifically humid air, dripping with sweat day and night. The clothing became damp and mouldy, and the water was lukewarm and stank; it was so revolting that the men had to hold their nose and drink it quickly in order to quench their great thirst. The dry biscuits on board ship and the other foods became infested with grubs, and it was a job to keep even one's eyes shut. Burning fever and splitting headaches causing delirium plagued most of the guests. Many regretted the day they set foot on the ship. The ship resembled a floating, but ill-equipped hospital. Nevertheless, Fr Mestre Francisco, or as the others usually called him, "the holy father", pulled himself together despite his own illness and helped the sick and dying. He refused to sit with the officers. He wanted nothing better than to be with the ordinary folk.

At last there was some wind again, but it was in the wrong direction. The convoy was driven towards Brazil, and it had to cross the ocean again with the new wind. In South Africa they discovered why that point was called "Cape of the Storms" at that time. Huge mountains of waves beat against the ship like waves against a barge. Since Bartholomus Dias sailed round the Cape for the first time in 1487 and changed its name to the Cape of Good Hope it had never lost its terrible reputation. The ships stopped for some time at Mozambique. Francisco worked in the hospital and listened to the accounts of the sick. He was then seized by a new illness himself which sent him into a delirium for three days.

Eventually the ships sailed on, and in the evening of May 14, 1542, the island of Queimadas was finally in sight. They were saved. Francis Xavier had to endure other similar journeys in ships and junks during his 10 years in Asia, journeys to Cochin, Sao Tome, Malacca, the Moluccas Islands and back to India, again to Malacca and Japan and back, finally to China, where he died on December 3, 1552, on the island of Sanzian, before the closed gates of China.

Even if the exaggerations and the ideals made by biographers about his life have recently been retold without making such a myth about it, there still remain enough positive resources to continually be able to include Francis Xavier as one of the great figures in the history of the missions.[4] It is easier to find fault with him than to imitate his actions. Nevertheless, one has to consider his limitations. He was a typical child of his time, and he thought and wrote about the Asian people and religions as was customary at that period of time: "The native Indians have no culture whatsoever ... . It is difficult to live amongst a people who does not know God, and who does not live according to its reasoning because it is so steeped in sin ...". Francis Xavier, the man of fervent prayer, did not perceive that he was in the most religious land in the world. On his journeys he was accompanied by a loyal servant, a pagan Chinese, who stuck by him even when the Portuguese deserted him. He regarded Francis as a brother. Unfortunately it never once crossed his mind to adopt his master's religion. Suddenly he died, and Francis Xavier wrote: "We could not reward him for his goodness of heart, for he died without knowing God. We could never help him or pray for him even after his death, for he is in hell". These are some of the harshest words to be said in the history of all times, and yet they came from such a kind and loving person! The prejudice was so deeply imbedded! His words on the Japanese were less harsh, but still he was critical about the bigwigs who, according to the people, tried to prevent conversion to Christianity. As regards his final proposed journey to China, he wrote to the King of Portugal and said: "We are going there to declare war upon the demons and the people whom they idolise. We have an immense mission from God to fulfil, and that is that they should no longer idolise demons".[5]

Another typical example of these historic heroes is Bishop Anastasius Hartmann (1803-1866), who came about 300 years later. When this Capuchin monk travelled to India in 1844, he needed another four and a half months to get to Alexandria from Rome by ship, then through the desert to Suez, and again by ship to Bombay, and eventually to arrive at Agra with his train of oxen — not to mention his many pastoral journeys which, again with a train of oxen, led him through a good half of what is known today as North India.[6] One could praise him for his devotion, his holiness and his farsighted missionary undertakings. But as far as his thoughts on paganism were concerned, he spoke the same language as the holy patron of the missions, i.e., the line of thought remained unchanged from the sixteenth to the nineteenth centuries.

When in 1841 he preached his final sermon in his local parish of Hitzkirch, he solemnly declared: "God is calling me from my native country, he is calling me out of Europe into a strange, unknown land far beyond the ocean, to be with wild people who live in the darkness and shadow of death, and I shall have to preach the gospel to them ... . I am leaving you and going to live amongst those wild people for one reason only, that reason being

21

to tear them away from final damnation and to save their souls by the light and grace of the gospel". When he arrived in Agra, he recorded his first impressions again: "The education of this people is at rock bottom and they practise the most base idolatry; what they need are the fundamental principles of community life, namely loyalty, honesty and an incentive to work. They were told that from one end of India to the other". On the basis of his own experiences, he even attributed to the pagans an invincible pride against their inertia and unchastity and their lack of feelings for anything spiritual or religious. He wrote that "the fakirs, with their black hair of the chieftains, their eyebrows, their beards, and their gleeful, haughty and fiendish looks seem almost devilish".[7] We would like to believe that Anastasius had not written such words, but that he had managed to discover God throughout his great search for a solution and purification amidst the incomprehensible customs, and even by the mistakes and distortions of paganism. Apart from that, whilst he came to independent conclusions about many issues, and became a pioneer of a number of modern ideas on missionary work, he was a child of his time and started to say the same things which were being spoken in the whole of Europe and especially throughout all the African and Asian colonies.

Just as derogatory judgements were made about India, similar ones were made about China. In 1876 a missionary in China summed up his opinion on the people and their religion: "The religions in China are ugly, absurd and the most ludicrous in the world ... the standard of art is non-existent, it has no expression, no aestheticism; their music is satanical, and they have not the faintest conception of beauty. The literature is stupid and childish, and empty, without any feelings; they are merely chanted words that make one sick".[8]

This awful speech still lingers into our century, and is repeated, for example, in the exclusive work of L. Kervyn on the apostolate in modern China.[9] A person like J. Beckmann who knows the history of the missions so well adds: "Works such as this one are typical neither of this Belgian missionary, nor of the missionary community to which he belonged, not even of the Catholic missions, but of the average European".[10]

We simply have to admire all these missionaries for their courage and ardent convictions, but nevertheless they have not been able to overcome the spiritual clefts between Europe and Asia to the same extent that they have overcome the geographical distances. They have remained profoundly European. They can only see non-christian religions through the filter of their own prejudices. There was nothing here for them to discover or to recognise, only something to judge, or at the most, to conceal graciously, and at the same time to do everything possible to save these souls from their hopeless plight.

Is it no wonder that when such comments about the Asian religions and cultures are made, a last echo rebounds and the Asian people, who today have far more freedom of speech, attack the methods which we have employed in our missionary work? Twenty years ago Thomas Ohm took the trouble of collecting such voices of opinion to make us aware of what the Asians thought about our missions. They said that Christianity meant the renouncement of all other religions and the violation of spirits; as such, it was unfounded, senseless, foolish and inhuman. It was more like religious imperialism. For that reason even the christian attack on Hinduism, Buddhism and Islam remained a total mistake. The few people who had been converted were no reason for the missions to boast, for what was really at stake were the poor and needy, the farmers and the uneducated. The missionaries had judged the religion without really knowing it, and continually talked about the "worship of idols" and "the worship of more than one god"; they brought back to Europe horrifically distorted pictures of the Asian religions. Numerous other accusations were made, but we shall limit ourselves to those which are concerned primarily with Asian religions and cultures.[11]

23

Now, what is surprising and significant is that even Thomas Ohm, who in so many books and articles had always been in favour of a better understanding of Asia, was basically not courageous enough to break down the barrier. Fixed in his christian conviction, he remained loyal to the categorical assertion that "as a whole Buddhism, Hinduism and Islam are in no way God-willed or God-given religions".[12] Despite all the wonderful things he said in his collected works about God's love in the non-christian religions, only with some degree of hesitation did he raise the question as to whether it was quite unfounded to assume that God's grace is present in this faith, hope and love, and that the God-willed seeds of a future supernatural life have been sown. On the other hand, he pointed out equally that many theologians disagreed on this opinion, and that they believed that true supernatural mystique was assumed by faith in the Trinity and redemption, or that these necessarily led to the faith.[13]

"All those religions come from the devil and lead back to the devil", is what has been continually said throughout the centuries; "these religions have nothing to do with God and are not included in the sphere of his grace", is what theologians stated only 20 years ago: is this where we have to stop? Cannot we really try to jump ahead of our christian shadow? Or are we perhaps dancing with a shadow which originates from Christians but not from Christ? Gandhi asked himself this question in 1939. Is it possible that by his answer God also spoke to us without our realising it at that time? This is what Gandhi said about the situation of the christian missionaries in India: "Until then they came to us as teachers and preachers with odd ideas about India and the Indian religions. We were described as a land of superstitious pagans who knew nothing about God and who denied God. We are a brood of Satan, as Murdoch would say. ... I am convinced that to say that is a denial of the Spirit of Christ ... . What you find difficult is that you look upon other religions to be wrong or you mar them to such an extent that they equal falsity. You shut your eyes before the truth which shines in the other religions and which give its believers true joy and peace. Therefore I did not hesitate to recommend to my christian friends a study of the other holy scriptures of the world, along with prayer and sympathy. From my own experience I can say that a study like this enabled me to pay tribute to them as well as to my own religion. It has enriched my personal faith and has broadened my horizons ... . Stop thinking that you have to convert the whole world to your interpretation of Christianity. Let me tell you that after I read the Bible I could not get out of my mind the impression that Christ never expected from Christians, or what the majority call themselves Christians, what they are doing now".[14] He added that if people wanted to foster dialogue as a new, inter-religious code of behaviour, there would always be room for missionaries in India.

How true is Gandhi's analysis? To what extent has the development put him in the right? Just how far has the new era of dialogue taken its promising roots in Asia? The reporter's journey begins through the last 20 years of Asia in search of the answer to all these questions.

3

The Leap Forward in the Vatican

OUR first stop is not on the periphery of Christianity, in Asia, but at its very centre, in the Vatican, where the Council has been sitting in conference for a year. We are in the second half of 1963. In the Council Assembly Hall ideas on ecumenism, non-christian religions and religious freedom are still being put forward without any particular order — intuitively, spontaneously — dynamic ideas which question former ways of thinking. But without these ideas the later conferences in Asia, which we shall be visiting, would have probably never happened. In order to measure the implications of these ideas, one has to set them against the background of the style of the Roman Curia, which was customary until the threshold of the second Vatican Council. For it was not only the missionaries who reflected the opinions of the times in their derogatory judgements about the non-christian religions. Even the Vatican until then had not yet struggled towards its own prophetic interpretation. It is illuminating to browse through the documents and speeches made by the immediate Popes before the Council concerning this point of view.[15]

Benedict XV: "An enormous number of souls must be saved from the proud tyranny of Satan and be brought to the freedom of the children of God. ... In their misunderstanding many people are still very far away from the true faith ... . What type of people needs brotherly love more than the non-believers who do not know God at all? Bound by blind, unrestrained passions they languish in the worst possible slavery, that of the domination of the devil ...".

Pius XI: "One of the greatest and most wonderful signs of love for one's neighbour is when, by our loving care, the pagans are led out of their murky superstitions and are filled with the true faith in Christ ... . No one is as poor, naked, ill, hungry and thirsty as a person who does not know God and who lacks his grace ...".

Pius XII: In his encyclical on the missions entitled *Evangelii praecones* (1951) he still actually uses the expression "pagans", yet otherwise he speaks about the different cultures and religions with great respect. In the *Fidei donum* of 1957, however, he falls back into the old style and mentions that "still about 85 million black Africans worship their heathen gods". From then on he refrains from using such terms.

But the real breakthrough followed with John XXIII and Paul VI. It would be interesting to trace when, how and why this change came about. Even John XXIII had earlier thought along the conventional lines, as is apparent from his diary. Who is responsible for imparting these new ideas to him?

Obviously there were people who, centuries ahead of the times, tried to gain some insight into the religions and to interpret them: ethnologists, theologians and even a number of missionaries. We only have to think of the 12 volumes of Professor W. Schmidt's *The Origin of the Idea of God,* in which he collected material on the religions of the people of ancient times and of the African and Asian farming folk. Today, libraries are full of literature on the Asian high religions.

Even early on, individual theologians came up with this contemporary conception — if that is what you want to call it — simply by reflecting upon it in an unprejudiced way. Cardinal John H. Newman (1801-1890) stands out as one of them. In accordance with the church fathers, especially with the school of Alexandria and Augustine, he believes that there is something to be revealed in every religion in the whole wide world, and that the heathen writers were also inspired by God. Certainly this kind of revelation is not recognised officially. Yet it is "a great comfort to believe that God's grace is not limited to the boundaries of its legacy, but rather that anyone within or outside the Church who calls upon the name of God with a pure and contrite heart will be saved ...". As a reward from Christ "grace can be bestowed upon the whole earth at his will; there is no corner, not even in paganism, where the grace of God is not present; it exists in every person's heart to a truly sufficient extent for his final salvation ...". W. Henkel, who published a study of this attitude of Newman, sums up: "If, according to the Bible itself, all knowledge of the religion of God is the same, and not only that which the Bible mediates, then one has to come to the conclusion that the religions are legitimate. That does not mean to say that they are not lacking in something, as Newman did in fact point out, but that they are means towards salvation ... . This is why the pagan religions should be taken seriously in their social context in which the religious opinions come to light. On the whole they are the expression of the relationship between God and man, which serve as a way towards salvation".[16]

Another pioneer was O. Karrer (1888-1976). He followed in the wake of Newman, whose ideas he developed further, and produced a systematic showpiece. In 1934 he published his sensational study on the non-christian religions.[17] This was certainly not done out of the desire to cause a sensation, but it happened because of an alert sense of the signs of the times. He could see how the times and the ways of thinking were changing, and portrayed them so clearly in far-sighted perceptions, that one could be excused for thinking his work was written in this decade. He wrote that the progressive enlightenment of most social classes through ethnology and theology, and by means of travel, radio and literature brought closer even those who were furthest away. At the same time one had to be introspective and undergo a psychological discovery in order to become clear-sighted about the subjective requirements for the humane spiritual life. By this process, the question of the religious in mankind and the relationship between Christianity and the other religions has become perhaps one of the most exciting in christian discussion. Protestant liberal theology had already solved this question by forsaking the absolute claim to Christianity. It was at the time that Catholic theology posed this question whenever it did not want its own dogma to be suddenly shattered by theological developments. As in sexual matters, the explanation here should not be left to just anyone, if one does not want to risk devastating harm. The problem must therefore be approached "at the point where these questions press every thinking person most. For these questions lie at the core of the matter, and this core belongs to God. To avoid the issue means not wanting to see God".[18] The problem is now being presented on the basis of a wealth of historical religious, philosophical and theological literature, and an almost dangerous attempt is being made — at least it appears dangerous to a traditional believer — to fathom out the seeds of truth in the non-christian religions and to measure the validity of those religions in their relationship with supernatural truth. Karrer's book fulfilled a true need and made a breakthrough — which meanwhile, of course, few people followed.

But now we are in the Vatican Council, which was somewhat delayed, although to not too great an extent, in taking the leap forward. Three great openings were attributed to this historical meeting of the Churches: the opening to the lay people, to the Christians and to the non-Christians. Nowadays, however, it is thought that John XXIII and his closest colleagues had not previously set this aim for the Council. On the contrary, one is struck by how the theme of different religions came to be discussed "by chance" in St Peter's — a Christian would say that it was obviously not inspired by the individual but was led by

29

the Spirit of God! John XXIII had only one conviction, and that was that the enmity between Jews and Christians should be buried once and for all. That is why he gave the Secretariat for Christian Unity also the task of working out a schema to solve the problem of the Jews. But then it was decided by the majority that the Arabic states might consider the text too sympathetic towards the Jews, and it was therefore removed. However, the idea itself was put forward on the intervention of Cardinal Bea in November 1963 as Chapter IV of the Schema on Ecumenism.

In relation to this, quite unexpected voices piped up and declared that if the Council was going to talk about the Jews, something ought to be said about the non-christian religions as well. Among others, Bishop F. Da Veiga Couthinho of Belgaum in India made an address on November 22, 1963. He was from Goa, tall and intelligent, a former student of Louvain, who knew how to tread and command respect. He declared: "In connection with ecumenism in missionary countries it is of great importance that attention should also be paid to the non-christian religions, that is to say that the Council should also be concerned with them. A schema which speaks only about the Jews and not about the other religions is therefore an unsatisfactory one. In all probability, this text will be falsely interpreted, on the one hand by the Arabic states for political reasons, and on the other hand by Asia, a land of old religions which have never once seemed worth talking about in the Council. One should either remove it from the chapter on the Jews, or add different chapters concerning Islam, Hinduism and all the other religions which have millions of followers. We must present the unity of the plan of salvation for the entire human race in a clear way, and we must emphasise the fact that everyone has a place in God's plan. The old cultures must be regarded as paving the way for the truth of the gospel, and the religions must be portrayed with great respect. If we do not want to close the doors upon a spirit of understanding, we too must finally reject all slanderous expressions against those who follow another religion in good faith, and we must no longer talk about the 'darkness of ignorance, paganism, worship of idols' etc".[19]

This logic hits home. It is supported by Bishop Hoa Nguyen-van-Binh from Vietnam: "How often it is pointed out to enforce respect and goodwill in the face of non-Christians, for all are called upon to be a part of the Church whilst the majority of the world is not made up of Christians. One should draw near to these non-Christians without possessing any feeling of superiority whatsoever, and one should not arrogantly rebuff the positive values of their culture. Anything which could injure the honour and dignity of those people to whom the word of God is going to be spoken should be rejected from the Catholic press, and especially the missionary press. One must avoid giving the impression that whoever is not a Catholic will automatically go to hell. Salvation depends upon the grace of God, upon his invitation and the answer that the individual gives". He too stands by his word that he will discuss all religions or that he will say nothing about the Jews.[20]

Other bishops also followed suit, and so a schema on the non-christian religions was ordered. Then it certainly went through a very changeable history, until finally it was adopted on October 28, 1965, under the title "Declaration on the Relationship of the Church to non-Christian Religions". For all that, in the course of two years there prevailed a development of awareness which previously had scarcely existed; new horizons opened within the official Church, horizons which had earlier been embarked upon only by individual pioneers. The level-headed K. Rahner said that "the declaration was unique in its text and in its inner potential of the history of the Church, of its Councils and of its theology".[21]

A similar story applies to the declaration on religious freedom. This text too was first of all — just as the idea of the Jews and the non-christian religions — to be an appendix to the Schema on Ecumenism. Then it received its independence, but it had to fight against strong winds

31

of opposition until it arrived in the harbour of the Vatican Council as the final document. In this way, talks on these three issues overlapped in those November days of 1963.

On November 19, Bishop E. J. De Smedt from Bruges in Belgium made a speech which ranked as one of the most significant ever made in the Council, and which laid the firm foundations not only for the subject of religious freedom but also for dialogue with the other religions.[22] A man of medium height, De Smedt acts as an exponent of a dynamic Church. His pastoral letters are widely read and fill people with inspiration. He argued: "Numerous fathers of the Vatican Council have urgently desired that this Council should clearly explain and publicise people's rights on religious freedom. There are principally four reasons for this demand: 1) the motive of truth; the Church must defend the right of religious freedom for it is an act of truth; it has the duty to preserve it; 2) the motive of defence; today the Church cannot remain silent in a world where almost half the human population is deprived of religious freedom in varying degrees by means of an atheistic materialism; 3) the motive of peaceful co-existence; nowadays, in every country of the world, people who profess different religions and even people who do not follow any religion are being called to live together in one and the same society; in the light of truth the Church must provide a meaningful road in life for them; 4) the motive of seeking world-wide christian unity; numerous non-Catholic Christians are approaching a certain aversion to the Church, or they suspect it of a certain Machiavellianism because it demands religious freedom in countries where Catholics are in the minority, yet it treats this freedom in an underhand way ... ".

The speaker then declared that religious freedom should not be equalled to indifference, and he asserted positively: "Religious freedom is a person's right to the free practice of his religion according to the conviction of his conscience ... . Catholics must restrain themselves from every other direct or indirect pressure. Even if it is God's will that the entire human race should be saved and should know the truth, Christ's followers are not allowed to strangle the religious freedom of another person. On the contrary, they must follow their conscience and recognise and respect the rights and the duties of another, even if that conscience is at fault after a sincere examination of good-will". What he used to say previously to non-Catholic Christians he now extended to all people: "The human person who is able to behave in an aware and free manner cannot fulfil God's will unless he recognises the divine law in the demands of conscience. He cannot therefore reach the ultimate aim if he is not careful in formulating the judgement of his conscience and being able to follow it loyally. By its sheer nature no other person nor any human institution can replace human conscience ... . A person who really follows his conscience wants to obey God himself, even if his conscience is perhaps confused and unaware. Such a person must therefore be approached with great respect. Whoever violates religious freedom also violates the freedom of the individual in a sphere of the utmost importance. That in itself is a thing of gross inequality".

In addition to this is linked the right to express publicly one's innermost thoughts and to practise religion in society. Only when the rights of another person or the well-being of the community are disrupted can the state authorities intervene.

The speaker then went on to point out the principle of continuity and progress in the attitude of the Church to this question from Pius IX up to John XXIII's *Pacem in terris*, for the Church always changes with the times and often when faced with false teachings it gradually finds the right teaching. *Pacem in terris* was for this reason like a ripe fruit, and was well accepted within and outside the Church as hardly any earlier document was accepted.

After the long speech he called upon the fathers: "We hope that it will be possible to settle the debate on this short, but extremely important, text before the end of this session. How fruitful our work would appear to the world if the fathers of the Council could, through the mouthpiece of the successor of St Peter joyfully proclaim the liberating doctrine of religious freedom".

Obviously things did not happen all that quickly. As mentioned earlier, the text had to persevere for two whole years, until as the declaration *Dignitatis humanae* the worthy conclusion was approved by all members of the Council. With this dynamic frankness on the subject of conscience, it expressed that in fact the Vatican Council had embarked upon a new life.

One has to admit, therefore, that on the basis of his human dignity and freedom, every person has the right and duty to live and act according to his conscience. This is not a vindication of a person's honour for non-Christians and non-Catholics. Within the Church one will also have to reckon with the fact that henceforth people will be going "their own way", and that even in the Catholic Church from now on there will be a greater multiplicity of forms and styles of life, and that — with the best of intentions — there will even be rebellion and divisions. These can no longer be quelled with the power of the Inquisition, but by rational talking and the force of conviction. Naturally this presupposes a new style of leadership at all levels in the Church, which will be marked more by animation rather than by authority.

Whilst such new ideas were fermenting and maturing in the Assembly Hall of the Vatican Council, they were also being made palatable to a wider audience via press conferences and interviews. Together with the bishops the people of the Church should endure the growth of an awareness, and should not suddenly be taken by surprise with the new ideas. And so, in those November days, Cardinal König from Vienna had an interview with Fr Gheddo which was published in *L'Osservatore Romano*.[23] Many journalists, however, pounced upon it and translated it for other countries. The Cardinal, a former professor of religious history and the editor of the well known handbook *Christ and the Religions of the Earth*, was called upon in a special way to give his opinion on this issue. As an introduction he affirmed that contrary to Vatican I, which remained the concern of the homeland, Vatican II had aroused interest all over the world, and that daily papers in Africa and parts of Asia gave more space to it than western newspapers did. He attributed that to the figure of John XXIII, and also to the fact that nowadays, more and more people were beginning to see that spiritual values were superior to everyday events. One had come to realise that modern life was not the road to happiness. "From this stems this almost messiah-like hope in something which will bring joy to all people, which will be able to answer some of the anxious questions posed by men and women, a hope which can no longer be found in the jungle of life". Then he went on to speak of the dialogue with the religions: "Our world, which once seemed so huge, has shrunk through modern developments. People and nations continue to grow closer to each other. It is therefore inevitable that one should meet not simply on political and economic levels, but also, and especially on cultural and spiritual levels ... . Whoever studies the history of religion, the idea that the human person is a 'religious animal', that the search for God is a basic feature of the human spirit — which is why there has never been a nation without a religion — will be very clear to him". He also confirmed that at the present time there exists a great interest in other religions. This was a good thing, he maintained, although one had to possess certain criteria when assessing them: before making a study of those religions, one had to have a better knowledge of one's own Christianity than simply from the catechism. "When one gets closer to those religions, he will affirm with what longing and passion a person will continually search for the truth about God, and how restless that person will be until he or she has found this truth". Certainly we should not neglect the fact that there might also be a lot of evil in those religions, and that in a certain sense they might be misleading paths. What the Cardinal wants is for our theologians and professors to be involved to a far greater extent with the problems of the other religions, and to bring the young people of today to this ecumenical spirit with its universal reach. "I believe that God's providence has brought to the people of today, and even more so to people of the future, the good fortune of recognising each other as brothers and sisters, to feel like children of the one God in heaven above all other division of race, tongue and culture. We must work with humility and trust in this direction, to try and bring that day even closer".

At the same time as the decree on the non-christian religions came into being, the idea of having a single Roman Secretariat for these religions also emerged. Just like the decree, this idea too experienced its hour of birth quite "by chance".[24] It happened in the following way. On April 2, 1963, Archbishop Jean Zoa from Yaunde, Cameroon, held a press conference to emphasise that in addition to the pastoral and ecumenical function of the Church, the missionary sphere should not be ignored. He said that the majority of the human race still remained outside the boundaries of the Church, and the first duty of the Christians was to go out to those people. Fr R. M. Wiltgen SVD, who was in charge of an international press agency, attended the conference. That evening in the chapel, he pondered over what he had heard, but had to admit to himself realistically that a large proportion of these people would in the meantime not let themselves be converted, but that on the other hand we had a lot to learn from them on a social and a religious level. The idea suddenly struck him to set up a Roman Secretariat in order to promote contact with those people and their religions. The next day his confrere Bishop A. Thijssen from Indonesia was won over to the idea. He then held a press conference on April 6 and made this request public. The following day he presented it to the Congregation for the evangelisation of peoples. The next question was how to proceed so that the idea reached the Pope.

Quite independently of Fr Wiltgen, in fact a day before

the inspiration of that evening, Cardinal Bea had expressed exactly the same thoughts in a press conference in New York. He, too, had said that the Secretariat for Christians could not be responsible for the very necessary dialogue with the non-Christians. What was needed was a single office to translate this far-reaching vision of making a family of man from the human race, for indeed everyone was created in the image and likeness of God for action. But the idea remained floating in mid-air. It required only prophets to come across it and to put in into practice.

John XXIII was at that time on the brink of death, and died on June 3. On June 30 Paul VI succeeded him. In the following month, the Chinese Cardinal Tien, a supporter of Fr Wiltgen, also wrote about him and his request in a letter addressed to the new Pope. This was immediately accepted, and already on September 12 he publicly declared that he intended to set up a Secretariat for the non-christian religions.

On May 17, 1964 at Whitsun, the Pope confirmed his decision, which, as he added, had the voice and the power of Whitsun inherent in it. On May 21 the aim of the new Secretariat was described in *L'Osservatore Romano*: it had arisen totally out of the Council's atmosphere of unity and sympathy among all believers (!) and was to serve towards mutual understanding, a sincere encounter and a working together in all possible spheres. How often had ignorance, prejudice and even the half awareness of a wrong faith made us enemies? We had only seen depravity on both sides, whereas a glimpse with a little more love would have revealed so much natural virtue. The Pope immediately emphasised that this central Secretariat could only have a limited task, and that any contact would have to be made, above all, outside the Church, on its periphery and in concrete situations by ordinary people.

Now, more than ten years later, we do not need to delve into the content of the declaration on the non-christian religions. It has been commented upon in enough books. It begins characteristically with the words *Nostra aetate*, i.e., "In our present day and age, where the human race is trying to unify itself from day to day, and where links between different peoples are increasing, the Church is considering with an even greater attentiveness how it stands in its relationship with non-christian religions". In this document the Church does not stress its understanding of itself and its missionary charge — neither of these aspects are questioned and are in any case discussed in other documents — but it does stress its other, equally important task, that of "advancing unity and love among peoples and thereby also between nations", and therefore "above all to consider what is common to humankind".

In all the new evaluations which were made, no conclusion was found. This was because the time it needed to be prepared and considered was far too short. The declaration spoke with great reverence about those religions, and recognised their values and also admitted the possibility of salvation of persons through them, but it did not pose the question of the salvation element of the religions as such; in other words, whether that person, *despite* his religion, or *in* it, or even *through* it could be saved. It was left as an unresolved question of post-conciliar theology.

Therefore the declaration and the new Secretariat do not constitute a conclusion, but a starting point, not a final act, but a prelude. Given the signal of the green light, one can now proceed along the new road. Those years — 1963, when the text on non-christian religions was demanded, 1964, when the Secretariat came into being, and 1965, when the declaration was accepted — all triggered off a whole new movement, a chain reaction. At present this subject matter is being taken up avidly everywhere. In autumn 1964 the well known Missionary Week of Louvain dealt with this issue, so too did the Missionary Study Week in Milan,[25] as well as a congress of theologians in Bombay, to which we shall come back later. In 1965 the *Bibliografia missionaria* of Rome felt compelled to start up a new line, namely "the scientific study of religion and mission", because it had overlooked missionary publications. Literature on this subject accumulated at a fantastic rate in no time at all. Henceforth it has also become one of the regular topics of discussion of the Holy Father. Missionary journals, which previously used to regard those religions as only an object of missionary zeal, and therefore portrayed chiefly the negative side, suddenly changed their tune and began to speak of the positive virtues of these religions in order to evoke the sympathy of the reader and to stimulate the devotion of possible professions. Meetings and conferences on all levels between Christians and non-Christians became a matter of course.

Truly, the declaration on the non-christian religions has broken down barriers. The result of this is that whereas these religions were previously like a stranger before a Christian's door, something to which hardly any attention was paid, rather like an enemy which one tried to kill, they gradually became a household friend with whom one could cultivate an exchange of thanks and experiences, without either partner having to disown his family or identity. It is without any shadow of a doubt, an enormous achievement to have found two-thirds of the human race, an achievement which is full of promise for co-existence in the one world.

4

Agitation Due to a False Alarm in Bombay

THE numerous participants from Europe and North America who came to the Eucharistic Congress in November 1964 were pleasantly surprised to find such a mild climate. Had they made the journey in May or June, they would have come sooner with their expectations — or fears — on account of the tropical heat. They were met with another surprise: tracts were being distributed in the streets, and menacing placards were being hung up. Was that the sign of the renowned hospitality of the Asians? A group of radical Hindus had done their utmost to disrupt the event, for fear of a missionary tide emanating from the Congress. The Congress office staff in Convent Street was apprehensive. However, the safety precautions taken by the government prevented more serious disruption.

When, on Sunday morning, 100,000 participants celebrated the "Statio orbis", the Mass which opened the Congress in the modest, but thoughtfully decorated oval, the religious enthusiasm of this minority seemed to have won over the interest and sympathy of the overwhelming majority. From then onwards, the Congress assumed the face and the atmosphere of a city with four million inhabitants. There were a great many on-lookers to be seen: Hindus, Parsees and Muslims. Silence, discipline and a religious atmosphere reigned; it was far from being a noisy, religious festival. Many voluntary helpers in the peace-keeping forces were Hindus, especially young Hindus. This event was the topic of conversation not only in Bombay, but the whole of India. Suddenly the Catholic Church did not appear to be so isolated and so much of a stranger as one thought. It had achieved a great deal in its road to recognition as a native, Indian religion which naturally raised the fears of radical circles to an even more intensive and feverish pitch.

The climax of the gathering was naturally the Pope's visit. There was a tightly packed crowd along the 25km route from the airport to the oval. Everyone wanted to see this "Holy Man" and to discover his power. He had a full programme for two days and met all groups of people: Catholics, other Christians, non-Christians and the poor. He avoided every pomp and ceremony and modestly called himself a "Pilgrim of Peace". When, on the Saturday evening he folded his hands to give the Indian greeting, and took his leave with a "Namasté" (Farewell), Bombay somehow became empty. For many, the Congress ended at that.[26]

Thursday, December 3, feast day of St Francis Xavier, holds a special significance for our context: right at the beginning of his programme, the Pope met representatives from Hinduism, Islam, Buddhism and Parseeism. Indeed, this is a symbol of a new era and a new dialogue! He spoke with such reverence for those religions, and everyone could see that it came from the depths of his heart: "This visit to India is the culmination of a desire which we have had in mind for a long time. Your land is the home of ancient culture, the cradle of great religions, the seat of a people which has searched for God with untiring zeal, in deep silence and awe, in hymns of intimate prayer. Seldom is such a holy longing for God marked with words so full of the Spirit of the coming of our Lord, as in the words of your holy scriptures, which, centuries before Christ, beseeched: 'Lead me from falsehood to truth; lead me from darkness to light; lead me from death to eternal life'. It is a prayer which belongs to our era too. Today, more than ever before, this prayer could be uttered from our very own hearts ... ".

The question is spontaneously raised why such texts could not be on a par with the Old Testament, and in certain circumstances why should they not even be read in the liturgy? This question will soon be posed in a very intensive way (cf. Chapter 9).

The Pope continued, "Today, the human race is experiencing deep-seated changes, and it wavers between basic principles which lead it in life, and between the new forces which will lead it into future life. Even your country has entered a phase in its history in which it is conscious of the insecurity of the present time, where the traditional systems and values are being toppled over. All possible forces must concentrate on building up the future of their nation, not only upon a material basis, but upon solid, spiritual foundations also. Even you are involved in this fight against the evil which enshrouds the life of countless people all over the world in darkness: the fight against poverty, hunger, disease; you, too, constantly fight to gain more food, clothing, housing and justice in the distribution of the world's goods. Are we not united in this fight for a better world, in this attempt to give to all people those riches which are necessary in making human destiny meaningful, and to live a life which is worthy of the children of God? We must therefore stand even closer together, not just via the modern means of communication of the press and radio, ships and jet planes, but also through our hearts, through mutual understanding, through reverence and love. We should not meet merely as tourists, but rather as pilgrims who come across each other on the way to their search for God, a God who is to be found not only in stone buildings but in the hearts of men ... ".

The emphasis of the speech, therefore, lies in the socio-political aspect: we are all in the same boat, we are a community of fate, and together we are building up a better — or a worse — world. Yet the motive for this joint task comes from above, from the common belief that we are all the children of God. In the second part, the Pope went on to mention that many million non-christian Hindus know and love Christ as an inspiration of love and self sacrifice, and he prayed that "God would awaken in all of us this love, and would bind us together as one with this invisible but indestructible bond which unites everyone, and which finds refuge in the love of God. May he make us all a family of his children".[27]

What the Pope did was to call up these non-christian comrades, to urge them not to simply revere Christ, but also to believe in him and to enter his Church. Protestant radicals reproached him afterwards for lacking the courage to witness for the missions. But this powerful speaker knew very well that discussions on the missions had their own time and place, and that one had to discern what was accordingly due by the signs of the times.

So far, so good! But in the middle of the Congress Reports an announcement made the rounds of the western press and worked like a false alarm which gave rise to lengthy, detailed discussions. The papers said that in Bombay, on the fringe of the Eucharistic Congress, a conference of Catholic theologians and professors had taken place, and that it had made the following declarations:

1) the classic definition "outside the Church no salvation" had to be categorically rejected;

2) Christ also revealed himself to people of non-christian religions;

3) the work of the missionaries did not consist so much of bringing salvation to the people, as making them aware of and officially ratifying Christianity, which already existed outside the christian Church;

4) the creation of the conditions which favoured the spiritual growth of individuals was more important than baptism;

5) where there was a large number of non-christian

children attending Catholic schools, they should also receive instruction in their own religion.

These were in fact unusual and provocative words. It is understandable that they evoked agitation in many circles. Fr Legrand[28] and Fr (later Cardinal) Daniélou became two of their strongest opponents. They were both pioneers of new pastoral methods and also of a new interpretation of the non-christian religions,[29] and they suddenly saw themselves being taken over by the "boys" and losing their place. Those five statements really did have a shocking effect. They could be misunderstood in their immediate and radical definition, but they did not necessarily have to be. Their purpose was not to reiterate the long-known missionary function of the Church; they expected mission when and where it was possible, but they wanted to tear down once and for all the barrier which had been put up over five centuries between Christianity and the other religions, and to pave a new theological path. Today, statements like these would cause less of a sensation, for in the meantime people have grown used to this way of thinking.

And now to the question: is that what the conclusions of the theological congress really were? What did, in fact, happen on the outskirts of Bombay in the Eucharistic Congress?

Because of the Eucharistic Congress, a theological meeting on "Christian revelation and non-christian religions" was called up, which took place from November 25 to 28. It was summoned on the initiative of the theological college in Pune, and especially through the enterprise of Fr Neuners. Doubtlessly it was a good idea. If one had the boldness to celebrate the focal secret of Christendom in a 97% non-christian country, then tact and theology urged one to talk about these Indian religions in a new way, to deepen the different insights, which were then being put through in the Vatican Council, and apply them in concrete situations and to preach them, in this continent of non-christian religions of all places. Previously, only individual theologians had expressed their opinion on those questions, but there had never been a theological conference.

On November 25, the hall of the Pius X Seminary in Bombay was filled with about 200 guests, a few theologians from the West, a lot of professors of theology from Indian seminaries, a number of bishops along with nuns and people of religious orders. The first step was to limit the Congress to inner-Church members. The press was not admitted because nobody wished to take any risks with such a delicate topic.

Professor Hans Küng was introduced as the first speaker. Who did not already know him? He made his name with great impact through his book on the doctrine of justification (1957) in which he showed that he understood how to break up some of the fixed ideas which people held, and to bring them nearer a solution by a completely new reflection based on the Bible. No less famous were his books on the structures of the Church, what the Church expects from the Vatican Council, truthfulness in the Church, etc. No doubt, Küng possessed the charisma to see old matters in new contexts, to search for a new theological answer to the latest facts in the world and to science, without fear of burning his fingers. As a speaker — whether in German, French, Italian or English, as was the case in this speech — he was an object of fascination because of his extraordinary eloquence and bold statements. Even today his talent shines. He and his colleague speakers make statements which are ahead of the times, but which in time, catch up with the times. They have not resigned themselves to standing still, but rather, they take three steps forward and one backwards, and so, bring the truth back on the right path again.

Professor Küng was to talk on the "world religions in God's plan of salvation".[30] He began his speech with the well-known axiom which has been repeated century after century, "No salvation outside the Church", and he con-

45

GOSHEN COLLEGE LIBRARY
GOSHEN, INDIANA

trasted this with a new — or a recently discovered — fact that out of two and a half billion people, there were only 500 million Catholics and all together 847 million Christians. In countries like China only 0.05% of the population was christian, and even in Europe a large number of the so-called Christians lived "outside the Church". How is this possible if we think of the past? The Bible calculates the span of the human race before Christ was 5200 years. Nowadays, this figure is estimated at over 600,000 years. We can pose the same anxious question about the future. The vast majority of humankind has always lived outside the Church and will continue to do so. Meanwhile, the missionary Church has no hopes whatsoever to change the situation, even less so as the favourable era since the age of discovery, during which Europe was predominant in all spheres, has come to an end, and every continent is on an equal footing, which is what would happen to the "western" religions too. Moreover, one can assert that the Asian religions have not died a slow death by their contact with western culture and religion, as most Christians expected; on the contrary, they developed a new, fresh strength. For them, the 400 years of the missions were obviously merely a phase in their much longer history, nothing more than a period of weakness which they then overcame. They are changing their attitude from a defensive one to an offensive one. They are being inspired towards "mission" by exactly the same dynamism of Christianity. "We become all the more aware that the axiom 'No salvation outside the Church' is not a good enough answer in this new direct competition with the great world religions. For the purposes of our discussion we need to realise that the theological question which is facing us today is not merely that of the individual persons outside the Church, but of those religions themselves outside the Church ... . Today, the theologian must seriously ask himself whether for someone, for whom Christ is not merely a matter of recovery but a new reflection on life, the revelation of Christ had anything positive to say about the salvation of the pagans, the old, long-standing ones as well as the new type — or as we prefer to say nowadays — the non-converted".

Küng then pointed out that the axiom "No salvation outside the Church" stemmed from an ecclesiocentric thought. The Church was compared to Noah's ark according to 1 Peter 3:20. Here it was positively asserted that salvation was possible in the ark and thereby in baptism, but there was no negative statement that the others would not receive salvation. The negative and exclusive interpretation only came about with Cyprian but it was never shared by the Church as such. Fulgentius a Ruspe, a pupil of the Augustinian school, was then very quick in formulating the critical phrase: "There is no doubt whatsoever that not only all pagans, but also all Jews, heretics and schismatics who die outside the Church will go into the eternal fire prepared for the devil and his followers". This view gave people a lot to talk about over the centuries, but a little door has still been left open for the idea of the "zest for baptism". The phrase itself was ambiguous and misleading. "Is salvation possible outside the Church? A true answer has to be 'Yes' or 'No', but not 'Yes' and 'No'." The speaker, therefore, suggested abandoning the phrase for practical purposes since it created more confusion than understanding. He then proposed the following axiom: "No salvation outside Christ". That would lead to a more theocentric way of looking at God. In fact, the God of the Old and New Testaments reveals himself as the God of all peoples and nations, and one could assume that this God has already saved people by his grace.

Küng then came to speak about the actual question of the significance of the world religions for the Church. He argued several theses:

— despite their truth, the religions were at the same time steeped in error and sin; consequently they somehow seemed ambiguous, and needed to be converted to the Lord Jesus Christ;

47

— the religions acknowledged God's truth. Whatever truth they had came from God and led to God;

— if correctly understood, they could be called the "usual path to salvation" for the non-christian people, whilst the Church could be called the "extraordinary path" because, in fact, far more people are saved through those religions and not through the Church. At all times and for all people everywhere God has been a God of salvation history, and the God of particular salvation history since Abraham and Jesus Christ;

— since God wanted to save the entire human race and to save every individual in his or her specific historical situation, "he sanctioned the religions as such as social structures. In different ways and at different levels they were legitimate religions. A person would be saved within that particular religion which was open to him or her in a certain historical situation. It was therefore that person's right and duty to search for God within this religion, in which the hidden God had already found that person ... ". Küng based these assertions on K. Rahner and H. Schlette;

— the religions taught the truth of Christ, even if they were mistaken in not recognising him as what he really is: the Truth. They could also hear the truth of Christ through teachers and prophets, and every positive virtue which they fostered was a virtue of Christ. He concluded the lengthy statement with two clear assertions:

1) "Every human being stands under the grace of God and *can* be saved, and we should like to hope that everyone *will* be saved".

2) "Every religion stands under the grace of God, and *can* be a path towards salvation, and we should like to hope that each one *is* a path towards salvation".

In one of the last parts of his speech he said the reverse about the significance of the Church for the other religions. He said that it should not merely enter into a peaceful co-existence with them, but that it should realise the necessity to live *for* them: the Church knew about the actual state of salvation of persons more than the other religions. It had to proclaim this publicly, and be united with the religions and their cares in order to foster mutual help. "What then is the Church's task amongst the world religions? The Church is not a privileged, exclusive club for those who are saved as opposed to those who are not. It is not the 'exclusive community of those awaiting salvation' but 'the historically visible vanguard ... the explicit embodiment, historically and socially constituted, of something which the Christian hopes is also given as a hidden reality outside the visibility of the Church'. It is, as Israel was, the *pars pro toto,* the minority there to serve the majority, the small number which represents the whole. It is — to use a phrase of Vatican I — the *signum elevatum in nationes,* the sign of the latter days, raised up amongst the nations of the world; the sign of the fulfilment of all things, which alone is the work of God and which is already visibly begun in it ... . The Church is thus the sign inviting the peoples of the world religions, so that from being Christians *de iure* they may become Christians *de facto,* from Christians *in spe* to Christians *in re;* that from being Christians by designation and vocation they may become Christians by profession and witness".

His lecture lasted a long time but it was not tiring. There was great applause. But the discussions showed that many people did not agree with everything that was said. Was it really that many, or was it only those that spoke up? Many people are still not used to such considerations. The type of language Küng employed was therefore particularly necessary to startle them from nodding off.

Professor Piet Fransen from Belgium has an equally good reputation for being a dogmatist. His teaching in Belgium, USA and Innsbruck, as well as his numerous publications are responsible for this. He pursued an additional question: *How* can non-Christians find salvation in their own religion?

First, he cleverly raised the point that the so-called "new" ideas were only new compared with unhistoric, abstract and therefore sterile theology, which had, after

49

all existed for a short length of time, but these ideas were much closer to the actual teachings of the Church than was commonly thought. He then presented these "new" and yet old interpretations of the effectiveness of the sacraments, of the dialectic movement of grace, of our historical existence before God, of the Church as an instrument of God, of the Lord of history.

He then continued by trying to find three ways to answer the above question. The first, well-known answer was the "votum implicitum Ecclesiae" (the implicit yearning for the Church), whereby one had to see the Church not as a human community and structure, but rather as a way to Christ, as a servant to the kingdom of God. The basic decision of the individual served as the second answer; it was a decision which he had to face again and again in his life, and which implicitly implied an act of faith and love, without which one could not be saved. The third way would now specifically apply to non-Christians. When a person gave up his basic decision for the highest virtues of his life, this did not happen outside the sphere of grace, for God did not abandon him in a "state of pure nature". "We think of the sincere, upright love and piety of millions of poor and simple folk, who are not in the position to delve further into the problems of religion, and who in the hour of their death have nothing more to ask of God. I am thinking of the simple, peaceful people in all these villages and provinces of this immeasurable country. The world does not know them, but God and his Spirit do. Only by following their conscience and the secret invitation of grace can they pursue the religious traditions of their fathers, as long as the christian faith does not illuminate their conscience and has not really entered their lives ... . Naturally, they retain from their traditions the more simple, popular forms of piety, which are often confused with idolatry, or years ago, with absurd, religious practices. The fact is that they simply do not know any other sort of religion. Christ died for them, just as he died for us, and he already sends his Spirit into their hearts. The Spirit of God beckons them to a greater love of God and their neighbour within their family and in the villages where they live. Whenever they listen to his voice and follow the supernatural impulses of grace, they meet God".

Fransen warned people against judging religions objectively and as an outsider because in this way one could not do justice to them. First one had to delve into them with every respect and sympathy, and then they had to be lived and experienced. But this could only be done if one accepted that Christ and his Spirit were already at work in these communities which are separated from us.

Then it was Joseph Masson's turn to speak. He was a professor in Louvain and in Rome. If this was the case, why was mission still necessary? Should we not rather leave those people in peace? This question was at the tip of everyone's tongue, and it was precisely the question which Masson had to answer. He could not help speaking, by way of introduction, about the crisis of mission, about the decline in missionary vocations and about so much confusion in matters concerning the missions. "The theologians have no right to air their theories if we cannot at the same time give a logical, satisfactory answer to the anxious question of the heroic and weary missionaries or to the doubts and hesitations of young people about their vocation to the missions". He then went on to show how the Church, through all its understanding of itself, was a missionary Church, but that it never forced itself nor its teachings on to people; rather it offered them. Precisely because the non-Christians, in so far as they were people of goodwill, already belonged to Christ, they had to be made aware of his existence and the fullness in Christ had to be offered to them. In order to justify his argument even more, he revealed the shortcomings of those religions. "People who prepare the way of the Lord will always be extremely necessary in the Church. These people will be the missionaries, now and forever, in good and in bad conditions. They are just as significant and effective as the love of God in Christ for all people through the Church".

Respect of the non-Christians and devotion to them should therefore go hand in hand. These two attitudes were complementary.

Without any shadow of doubt, this voice moved many hearts. Moreover, none of the other speakers ruled out mission. From now on mission could proceed without the fear of hell, but with a greater love towards God.

Everyone awaited Raymond Panikkar with great interest. He was an Indian world-priest who gained academic degrees in Spain, Germany and Italy in chemistry, philosophy and theology respectively. He has not only written a good number of books on the encounter between Christianity and Hinduism, but he also made an attempt to experience this encounter in his own body by meditating for two to three hours every day in his apartment in Varanasi, the holy town on the Ganges, and despite his amiability he would not allow anyone to disturb him during this period. His theme of discussion was the teaching of Christians in their non-christian surroundings.

Panikkar said that in the past, followers of different religions had by a certain instinct avoided contact with each other, as though they feared that their faith would be harmed. Nowadays, an attitude like this could no longer exist, neither in theory nor in practice. He then immediately defended himself by taking up the term "non-christian religions". It was an insult for these religions to be labelled simply with a negative criticism. Yet for us Christians there have never been any people or religions who had not already had some relation to God. The statement in the title, "non-christian surroundings", had therefore to be understood as a world in which Christ was not yet explicitly recognised as the Lord. Christians did not have the monopoly on Christ. On the contrary, they were the conscious fellow workers of Christ in his creative, redeeming and exalting actions in the whole wide world. Christian faith, hope and love did not create a barrier between God and the world; quite the opposite, they lived in the same light. The action of the Christian in the world was therefore totally without any purpose. What was necessary was to believe in God, to hope in him and to love the world in him in a theological act towards the world. "Only with this fundamental christian approach can the creeping discouragement, which hits the majority of missionaries, be overcome … . For a time a wrong and bitter zeal had been at work; a zeal which hindered true christian freedom and cut off christian peace".

Since Christ was the Alpha and the Omega of all creation, every being, especially every person, was like a Christian; no true human relationship or love was possible without Christ. This led to the conclusion that the most intimate human relationships only took place on a religious level, in the "communicatio in sacris" (which, without further ado means a total participation in the religious rites of the other religions). We could not simply limit our relationships to something profane. Each human relationship was *already* a religious one. Thus the true "koinonia" (community) was created through and beyond the "diakonia" (service) which did not exclude the "kerygma" (proclamation), which naturally had to happen primarily through one's own life in freedom and joy. The Eucharist that we celebrated always took place as a representation for the whole of humankind. The Communion we received was not merely an act of private devotion but a cosmic act. The relationship of the Christian to the "non-christian surroundings" did not initially consist of offering a new moral code of behaviour and new religious rites, but it was first and foremost concerned with the sacramental order that everyone was already sanctified by the sacramental actions of the Christians. "The Christians are channels of the Eucharist for those who do not receive it. The parables of Christ's kingdom and the function of Christians do not say that everyone should become Christians, but rather that his disciples should be the light, salt, seed and leaven which are there to bring light to people's lives, to provide a yearning, to die and to grow, to transform the entire mass of human beings".

Instead of giving some concrete advice as to what to do and what not to do, Panikkar put the relationship of Christians to non-Christians in a completely new theological light. In the discussion, specific questions — understandably so — were naturally directed at the speaker: how far should one participate in certain hindu rites; to what extent should one give Catholic schools the opportunity to allow hindu students to practise their religion? ... . No positive conclusions were reached.

On the last night the four speakers summed up in a joint debate a few points from the discussions for each lecture. They clarified themselves and corrected each other. Hans Küng showed that in no way was he a stubborn man, and consented to change his assertion that the non-christian religions were roads to salvation to the following: "For the person who is not confronted with the gospel of Jesus Christ in an existentialist way, these religions *can be a channel* for the grace of the salvation of Christ". Later, the four pages were presented before the plenum and were accepted as the "Declarations of the Conference" with a two-thirds majority. On the whole, there was a very good atmosphere during the congress. People did not split into a right and a left camp; they respected each other's opinion, and nobody doubted each other's loyalty and love for the Church. Everybody lived in the spirit of the Eucharistic Congress. As the first congress on this delicate theme, Bombay stood the test well in 1964.

The story of that "false alarm", which sparked off so much panic amongst some people, remains to be clarified. After the Eucharistic Congress, Professor Küng gave a few more lectures there and then, and had obviously interpreted the viewpoints of the Congress of Theologians with insufficient shades of meaning. In turn, edited, radical formulations reached the press as "statements made by the Congress". Both sides were in the wrong: first, the side which transmitted the misleading information, and secondly the side which did not wait for the official declarations of the Congress, but reacted very sharply to a news item. Today that is all forgotten, but the "original sin" of the post-conciliar period has not yet been removed from the Church. The sin was to have pushed some people forward in an unpsychological way whilst pulling the others back in an unchristian way, and thereby causing a polarisation within the Church. The forbidden fruit, which is eaten, is a self-confidence and complacency of the progressive circles and a narrow-minded, anxious view of the conservative circles. If both these groups were to listen more to the Spirit, they could avoid the polarisation and enjoy the fruits of the Spirit: love, peace, joy, patience, goodwill, kindness and forbearance (Gal 5:22) and thereby serve towards creating unity.

5

The Protestants Recover Lost Ground in Beirut

AFTER the meeting of the theologians in Bombay in 1964, there was a certain calm — the tranquillity of reflection or the lull before a storm, who knows? — until suddenly in 1970 some very important conferences came on to the scene. This time they were no longer merely concerned *about* the religions, but actually took place *with* representatives of those religions. It all began with the dialogue of the world religions from March 16 to 25, 1970 in Ajaltoun near Beirut which was organised by the World Council of Churches.[31]

The protestant Churches, of all Churches, took the initial step right into the religions. It felt a great need for recovery. The Catholic Church was far more advanced than the Protestant Church with a new interpretation of religions, a situation which threatened to create a further friction between the Churches. Now it has caught up with the Catholic Church, if not overtaken it. One must know the past history of this case.[32]

Indeed, there were also in the protestant Church pioneers in the sense that we understand today, for example, Nathan Söderblom, R. Otto, F. Heiler and P. Tillich. The liberal protestant theology in those days shot way beyond its aim and thereby even incurred the inexorable protest of the skilful bible interpreter, Karl Barth, who at that time exercised great influence not only over his pupils but also in the World Council of Churches, especially over H. Kraemer.[33] According to his dialectic theology the revelation of the "wholly other" God in Christ comes down vertically from above, and fails to find anything at all in the individual and his deeds which could serve forever as a basis or a starting point. The whole human existence, together with all the ritual manifestations, is subjected to the godly "No", and has cause for hope only in the "Yes" to the free, merciful choice in Jesus Christ. Religion is not a search for God; on the contrary, in religion the individual projects himself as God into heaven. Religion is a self-deification of the individual, "a powerless, stubborn attempt to create a substitute for God for oneself". In its mission, therefore, the Church must go out of its way to reach that group of people which thinks along those lines, which "is caught up in so many erroneous, random, powerless faiths and so much wrong, only because of its own glory and misery reflecting gods …".

This overruling judgement made by the teacher resounded in a dozen echoes with his successors. For example, according to J. Witte the pagan religions are "defection from God, a denial of God, a rebellion against God, an error and aberration, guilt and dejection. They are a delusion without any truth, they do not even bring anything as a first step or a preparation towards salvation, but lead ultimately to dejection". At that time in the World Council of Churches, only antithesis, discontinuity and a radical new beginning for those who accepted the gospel were the matters talked about as regards mission.

When the Catholic theologians then came along with a completely different interpretation, which was partially accepted in Vatican II, a certain uneasiness was aroused within protestant circles. On January 4, 1967, the German Evangelical Missionary Council published a document on the relationship with the Roman Catholic Church, in which a person, in fact, declares himself willing to the offered co-operation, but he makes the proviso: "We cannot hide the fact that we do not share the vision in which the Roman Catholic Church sees itself, and from which it determines its relationship with the world and the religions in the conciliar documents; furthermore, we cannot reconcile the gospel of the exoneration of the sinner. The presentation of the religions in the conciliar documents is biased ... . In our opinion, there can be no starting point of missionary preaching with available resources to those of non-christian religions ...".

It became increasingly evident that no progress could possibly be made with the protestant protest, especially now that in the World Council of Churches the voices of the young Church in Asia and Africa were being heard more and more, voices which were passionately interested in the concept of continuity. In order to work upon this problem, a large number of consultations and colloquies were organised.[34] A new way was being sought. In one colloquy in Nagpur in 1960, for the first time a few Hindus were invited. At the consultation in Kandy in 1967, for the first time there were Catholic participants. In 1968, Dr Stanley J. Samartha from India was called to Geneva to take charge of the enquiry into questions of mission and preaching, with the particular task of developing dialogue between religions and ideologies, a job which he undertook enthusiastically.

Thus the meeting in Beirut did not fall out of the sky like a meteor, but rather like a ripe fruit from a tree, after years of internal struggle and external contacts. It had now simply become necessary not to discuss dialogue any further, but to put it into practice. The event itself became an experience which surpassed all expectations. Dr Samartha quite rightly writes the following in the preface to the published document: "A collection of texts which were delivered at the consultation can no longer produce the warmth and liveliness of a personal meeting, just as a menu cannot produce the taste and aroma of a meal. However, it can whet the appetite and supply the material in order to acquire the worthwhile content of the lectures".

There were 38 people from 17 countries present. They were placed simply in alphabetical order on the list of participants, and not according to religious blocs. They consisted of 3 Hindus, 4 Buddhists, 3 Muslims, 6 Catholics and 22 Protestants and Orthodox.

At first, a hotel in the centre of Beirut was proposed, but then Dr Samartha pointed out in a preparatory visit that the hindu and buddhist monks could hardly feel at home in a mundane hotel room and restaurant. He then ferreted out near Ajaltoun a secluded hotel with a row of bungalows exclusively for the use of the consultation which would make a monastic type of existence possible. The decision was promptly made. It was wonderfully situated by the Mediterranean, a sea which represented the centre of the world for such a long time, near to the famous Nahr-el-Kalb, the gateway of invasion of so many conquerors in the Middle East and in Asia, near to the cradle of all the great religions, and at the same time situated "between" East and West: a more meaningful place for such a meeting could not have been found.

In the course of Sunday, March 15, the guests arrived. A few already knew each other personally, but the majority of them did not. However, the common religious basic attitude, the common great expectations, together with English as the unifying language quickly weaved together the necessary threads. The conference began on Monday. Already, that same day, the participants experienced the first practical ways of living together as a community. Both buddhist monks from Ceylon (now Sri Lanka) used their coffee-break at 11 a.m. to eat their lunch, for according to the rule of Sangha the main mealtime had to take place before midday. In the late afternoon about 6 o'clock, when the sun would begin to set over the Mediterranean, the president noticed that he had brought the muslim partners into a situation of conflict because they had to say their prayers before sunset. These were events which one noticed. The situation was not dissimilar to that of a married couple who have to adapt to each other.

Surprisingly — and understandably so — on the evening of the first day, Dr Askari, a Muslim, professor of sociology at the Osmania University in the Indian province of Hyderabad, asked why, despite the common bond of the whole day, they had not yet prayed together. As a result it was revealed that the Muslims had the least objection to common prayer. The Hindus, Buddhists and Muslims also sat in the room whilst Holy Communion was being celebrated, partly out of curiosity, partly in awe and for the experience of a wonderful secret. The Christians seemed to have great difficulty even at different levels to identify themselves in prayer with the others. A common Mass had been ruled out in advance.

Yet let us now turn to a few samples from the numerous lectures. All the speakers had borne in mind that this was not a matter of instructional talks, nor even classical religious talks of the post-Reformation era, but it was concerned with an introduction to dialogue. The Catholic hindu specialist, Fr K. Klostermaier, reported some practical experiences which he had had with christian groups on "inner dialogue". Before entering into dialogue with others, one had to prepare oneself for it from within, to free oneself from prejudices, and not to express theological considerations immediately, but to stride ahead towards the way of spirituality. The Hindu who believed in God, he claims, is already an "imago Dei" (an image of God). He is to be loved "in Christ". Before one speaks to him or enlightens him, one has to listen to him, and to ask oneself what God has to say to us through this, his representation. We must read the Upanishads (the holy books of Hinduism) "in the light of Christ", in order to discover their "deeper significance", to find Christ in them, just as it is possible to read about his presence in the Old Testament. And so the participants prepared themselves for the external dialogue, which included not simply theological questions, but the whole realm of life and history. Dialogue is not so much the meeting of Hinduism and Christianity as between individual Hindus and Christians, each professing his own faith. Dialogue stems, in other words, from a profound recognition of the mutuality of our common life. "In true dialogue there can be no feeling of superiority, nor any kind of indoctrination. It is a process of receiving and accepting ... . We are gratefully aware of the fact that in all types of dialogue there lies an inherent purpose, in so far as we can experience in and through this means of communication who God is, and what he can give to both partners. Dialogue is thus an experience of our most profound existence before God and our existence for others by the very nature that we are different from one another".

There then followed a number of reports giving some concrete experiences; a few were delivered as lectures, whilst others were distributed on printed sheets. It was obvious how intensively dialogue was already emerging at local levels. Groups everywhere were coming together for mutual exchange and common prayer. Masatoshi Dai, an eminent Christian from Japan, spoke about the relationship of dialogue and mission. He said that it was not possible to be satisfied with the simple theory of co-existence. Christianity was essentially a missionary religion. A lack of missionary enthusiasm was equal to a lack in true faith. The uniqueness of the gospel could not be ignored. Neither partner would even expect that; on the contrary their desire would be for Christianity to remain totally christian. Only in this way could it make its contribution to the spiritual life of the world. Conversion to Christianity is not made expressly for the purpose of dialogue, but the possibility of conversions or certain changes in the partner's opinion should not be ruled out, just as the Christians on their part must keep an open mind for the possibility of their viewpoint and ideas being changed.

On the basis of his own experience, Lynn A. de Silva,

61

a Protestant and the dynamic leader of the study-centre at Colombo and the journal *Dialogue,* came to the same conclusion, namely, that dialogue and mission do not exclude each other. Even Hinduism, Buddhism and Islam began as missionary movements, and they are becoming like that again nowadays. He declares that there must be understanding of mission which does not deviate from the conviction of one person nor abuse the trust of the other one.

Professor J. B. Carman from Harvard University creates favourable prerequisites for dialogue, but this in itself is not a substitute for dialogue. True dialogue, he maintained, does not occur on an intellectual level, but on the wave-length of the heart.

However, more important than all the lectures, documents and discussions was the atmosphere in which everyone breathed and lived during those ten days. It is remarkable that no one ever felt the need to go into the town for a break from the conference. Everyone felt inspired and satisfied. No word was ever mentioned against Rome. On the contrary, it was precisely this meeting with the non-Christians which produced in all the Christians, despite their differences of opinion, a very clear awareness of the unity in Christ. Equally, very little was mentioned about K. Barth and his theology. His conception was quietly dropped completely out of sight.

Towards the end, one representative from each of the four religions commented upon texts about religion and devotion; these texts can be included as some of the best literature produced on spirituality. The Hindu Swami Nityabodhananda said: "The interiority of faith, the spiritual nucleus in us, has its substance, the certitude that our inner-self reflects in some measure God's nature in its three aspects: God as a reality, God as Love, God as the ultimate Creator. This nucleus, desirous of higher and higher perfection, incessantly demands to be nourished by knowledge of God and God's love to me as revealed in the gospels of various faiths. It is a process by which man

62

pushes farther and farther his limits in order to annex his real heritage, God's resemblance ...".

The Buddhist Ananda Mangala Thera analysed at first the disintegration of religious values in modern society, especially in youth, yet he was convinced that true religion survived. He described his experience in the following words: "The sensual world of the human is left behind temporarily to enter into a realm of deeper vision and bigger dimensions through the experiencing of the divine eye and the divine ear. These great absorptions and the gradual development of such highly evolved minds lead to perfections and deeper spirituality. At all these levels people of faith meet on a common ground of spiritual joy.

"However, the over-enthusiasm of the mystics had often compelled them to burst into song in raptures of joy, attempting to describe such experiences transcending reason. Many have described the indescribable and made the herculean effort to speak — when in reality Silence alone should have been the answer ...".

The Anglican Bishop Kenneth Cragg put forward a subject for common devotion, which in every sense entailed certain sober thoughts. He claimed that one cannot escape the old maxim that an act of prayer means an act of faith. Common prayer was therefore the most dangerous of all undertakings. In common prayer one has to maintain self-possession, otherwise one's individualism will not be distinguished among the community. He continued by saying that obviously situations often arose where the starting-line is still in sight, but the final flag is far from view, where one feels urged to embark upon a moral obligation without having any clear idea of the aim or the consequences. The verdict can be left undecided for a certain time without interrupting the action. Yet one must really strive to discover the ultimate goal. Devotion should not become a "short-circuit dialogue", nor should it turn into a new romanticism as a counterbalance against secularisation. All this shows to what great extent we are still stuck in the sphere of ambiguity and shortcoming, something which should certainly not suffocate any creative solutions.

The Muslim Hasan Askari pointed out that it was not only devotion and dialogue which seemed paradoxical, but that among the devout the paradox is in no way to be shelved. One has to come to terms with this paradox-laden situation: the literal and the symbolic, the unity and the diversity, the mercy and the wrath of God, God as a being and "God in humankind", the close God and the absolute, intangible God. ... This is valid not only when experiencing God. In the religious experience, the believer turns to God as "another" being, whereas in the mystical experience a person undergoes absolute unity with God. This could well apply to the two concepts of dialogue and devotion. Dialogue still presumes the division that unity is achieved via some greater mystique. Mystical experience is not a prerequisite for dialogue, but it is one of its possible consequences. Through it, dialogue ceases. ... It was fascinating to listen to this learned, and yet so simple, explanation.

Initially, no one had intended to work towards a common agreement. It was more a matter of sharing experience, and not of coming to a final settlement and scholarly documents. Instead, a representative of each of the four religions was asked to write down his own impressions. These texts were published as a final memorandum. Their purpose was to express the diversity of ideas, the new, positive thoughts as well as some of the more tentative aspects. The overall viewpoint was very well presented in the introduction: "The keynote of the consultation was the understanding that a full and loyal commitment to one's own faith did not stand in the way of dialogue. On the contrary, it was our faith which was the very basis of, and driving force to, intensification of dialogue and a search for common action between members of different faiths in the various localities and situations in which they find themselves neighbours. This conviction was the presupposition of the consultation and was fully vindicated in a series of intensive and probing discussions which not only revealed many promising glimpses of agreements, but also brought out and made clearer disagreements in understanding the world and man's place in the world. Nonetheless the very disagreements were seen as points for further creative and intensive dialogue ... ".

The anonymous Hindu admitted, "Our dialogue during these days brings home to us a new dimension of theologising experience, viz., a felt sense of 'incompleteness', a sense of the need for the truly other — the 'other' in the way of thinking and feeling that I cannot simply assimilate my own, but which I confront inescapably, in other words, 'encounter'. ... It speaks for the recognition of a new source of strength, hitherto remaining undetected. By virtue of its very adequacy and relevance, it opens itself for looking beyond itself, and evokes in one a creative need for the other ...". Dialogue is not merely a process of coming together; rather, it is an act of sharing. The idea and the experience of a "caring" God, a feeling of godliness which is present in both my joys and my sufferings — especially in the unique experience of being a mortal — and also to be able to be a part of this christian experience: all these are truly a great gift.

The anonymous Buddhist wrote, amongst other things, that dialogue of this nature marked the end of an anti-inter-religious era, which tore down the barriers it had erected itself, and made it possible to prepare the way for the birth of a sincere friendship on spiritual and worldly levels between those of different creeds.

The anonymous Christian shirked from a positive conclusion mostly by asking questions which pointed out that a lot still remained open-ended. He said that in the future the abiding in each other in unity of the different creeds must signify a profound test as well as challenge of faith.

The anonymous Muslim confessed that it was impossible to put down in words the novelty of this meeting. Everyone had realised "that all together we are too small in the presence of God, simply too small to argue about him, and so there remains nothing to do but to submit ourselves, kneel and pray". It was in prayer that this feeling of togetherness was experienced most. Whoever led the prayers, whether Christian or Muslim, Hindu or Buddhist, was of no importance. Whether a Muslim said "Amen" after a christian prayer proclaiming Christ as the Son of God did not matter. The impression that everyone really experienced was the common human situation for God and in God. The most important outcome of the whole conference was not dialogue as such, but the experience of a special kind of community into which the participants were drawn.

Finally, it is significant to emphasise the fact that one no longer spoke of "non-Christians", but instead positive names were given to each individual: a Buddhist, a Christian, a Hindu, a Muslim. People did not speak about "religions" as systems and complexes with their many traditional and human elements, but rather as numerous "faiths", as creeds which automatically acted as a basis for dialogue: each individual acknowledges the legitimacy of the other's faith, just as I personally hold on to my own faith.

An event such as the one which took place in Beirut could not escape some consequences. Via its "Secretariat for dialogue with living faith and ideologies" the World Council of Churches organised from Beirut from 1970 until January 1975 a further 13 small and large meetings with each of the religious communities to discuss all the different aspects.[35] This Secretariat in Geneva, under the dynamic leadership of Dr Samartha, as well as the Vatican "Secretariat for the non-Christians" under the equally enterprising leadership of Cardinal Pignedoli and Mgr P. Rossano, became ice-breakers, so to speak, which made previously unattainable regions in God's world accessible.

Obviously, two swallows do not make a summer. Those two Secretariats cannot immediately break all the ice in their own Churches. The circle of followers around Professor

P. Beyerhaus, the "Frankfurt Manifesto 1970", the Kent Conference 1974, the Meeting of the Evangelicals in Lausanne 1974, etc. stand in opposition to this initiative of the World Council of Churches.[36] Ironically, one should not shy away from these circles, for they too have their function within the Church. Whenever the pioneers of dialogue grant their partner as much freedom as possible to enter into conversation, others have to ensure that we remain loyal to ourselves. The Churches need and tolerate both a right and a left flank which should not deny one another but should come to an understanding in inner-church dialogue.

One can assume that Barth's view of paganism gradually disappeared, not only amongst the leaders, but also amongst the protestant congregations. At least the new protestant adult catechism is carefully working in this direction. To the question of how people in other religions fare, it declares, "We can hope that there is a way to God for those people who do not hear the christian message, or who cannot accept it. ... A starting point towards the solution of this difficult problem of the other religions is offered by the New Testament when it speaks of Jesus as the 'Word of God', through whom all things are created. If everything *is* created through the Word, then there already lies in the creation an address to the people, for the fact that everyone is created means that each person has a link with God. Religions would then be the answer to this 'original revelation' of God. The old question: 'Can pagans reach heaven too?' does not therefore need to be answered in a negative way — as the above considerations are meant to show".[37] Of course, then the necessity to evangelise is unfolded.

In Beirut of all places, where this first breakthrough or this first meeting succeeded, the "Islamic World Congress" (Motamar al-Alam al-Islam) in December 1972, representing 570 million believers, examined publicly for the first time christian-islamic dialogue. It was established that out of all the religious communities these two were the closest to each other. Instead of both sides trying to preach to each other, they should come together to proclaim the message of God. Due to its identification with colonialism in the past, Christianity was brought into disrepute. This period of time had to be regarded as something of the past which ought not to burden the future. Since that December, the "Islamic World Congress" or the "World Muslim League" have expressed their views on christian-islamic dialogue six times. Efforts are being made to include the Jews in a "trilogy", and emphasis is laid on the fact that the "Arabic" world is not identical to Islam, for next to the 80 million Arabs there are a further half a billion people adhering to the islamic faith.[38]

6

The Religions Speak for Peace in Kyoto

DURING the discussions in the Vatican Council and the talks in Beirut, the internal theological and internal religious aspect was predominant. Now in Kyoto, however, it becomes instantly clear that the religions are placed as one before a gigantic, external task, the overcoming or not-overcoming of which is not only of decisive importance for humankind, but for the future of the religions themselves. Here in Kyoto, dialogue is assumed as a matter of course, not as the final outcome of theological reflection but as the postulate of practical reason and only the question is debated as to what the religions have to undertake in common and how they must proceed in order to unfold the way of peace for humankind.

Those very religions and confessions which for centuries argued with each other, uttered mutual condemnations and sparked off fratricidal wars, now offer each other their hand, in order to bring about peace among themselves and for the world. This is an event which cannot be denied importance in relation to world history and to the life and sufferings of Christ. This meeting showed how very differently we think today, even in comparison with a few decades ago.

The world conference of religions for peace, which took place from October 16 to 22, 1970 in the old, imperial, Japanese city of Kyoto,[39] originated in the suggestion of a small group of Americans and Japanese. After long discussions, they organised an American inter-confessional peace conference in 1966. This was followed in 1968 by an international and inter-religious symposium in New Delhi[40] and likewise in 1968 by a Japanese-American conference in Kyoto, where the plan for the world conference adopted its precise form.

The driving forces in these efforts were American theologian Dr Homer Jack and American lawyer Dr D. McLean Greeley, as well as several leaders of Japanese buddhist revival movements who had experienced together the atomic catastrophe of Hiroshima. Catholics had also contributed from the beginning: firstly Cardinal Wright, when he was still Bishop of Pittsburgh, and later Archbishop Angelo Fernandes of Delhi, who led the presidency in Kyoto.

The outcome of this conference becomes clear when compared to the one in Beirut where there were 38 people from 17 countries and 4 religions. Here there are 216 delegates from 39 countries and 10 religions (96 Christians, 38 Buddhists, 23 Hindus, 19 Shintoists, 18 Muslims, 7 Jews, 3 Sikhs and 2 Parsees — the remainder were distributed among smaller religious sects). Japan had the largest group with 53 participants. 33 came from India, 33 from the USA, 12 from the Soviet Union, etc. Unfortunately, the People's Republic of China was not represented. 107 observers and guests, 264 press representatives from all over the world and about 700 secretarial personnel and technical assistants accompanied the previously mentioned delegates. The organisation functioned perfectly, as can be expected from a highly industrialised nation like Japan. In addition, a further 2000 people from Kyoto and its surrounding district were invited to the opening and closing sessions.

Kyoto prides itself on being one of the most beautiful cities in the world. Is it, with its 1500 temples and shrines merely a nostalgic reminder of a religious past or is it a sign that secular Japan is basically not so secular after all? Nowadays, at any rate, the modern congress hall stands completely under the sign of the devout. The orange-coloured robes of the buddhist monks mingle with the silken garments of the Llamas from Mongolia, the multi-coloured, striped kaftans of the Muslims from Tashkent, the turbans of the Sikhs, the saris of the Indians, the kimonos of the Japanese, the solemn togas of the Greek Orthodox and the practical all-purpose clothes of the Americans and Europeans.

From the outset the Catholics have to come to terms with being described simply as "Christians" on the list of participants together with the Lutherans, Anglicans, Presbyterians, etc. Christianity, as a whole, is only valid here as one of the many world religions. One learns to make a virtue out of necessity and concerning the latter, to consider the present. In search for a common title for all those present, the new coinage, "religionists" is increasingly popular. All questions of precedence and theological reserves suddenly become secondary, if not insignificant, compared to the common external tasks and the same internal motives. In this respect, Kyoto will go down in history as the sign and symbol of religious emanci-pation and equality for all religions. This unity and equality also finds its expression in the morning and evening prayer-celebrations, which are organised by a different group in turn so that all participants can become acquainted with the different forms of oriental and western prayer.

After the documents were distributed in advance and thereafter taken for granted, one could be content with few speeches. Emphasis lay on the study-groups with the three objectives: disarmament, development, and human rights. Therefore, the common basis had to be laid in advance.

Archbishop Angelo Fernandes pointed out in the open-ing speech how in the last 25 years we had developed international co-operation as never before. One thinks of the programmes and efforts in the field of education and literacy, transport and communications, of overcoming starvation and diseases, and of political dealings in the interests of peace. That must not make us blind to the fact that all the awakened hopes were only fulfilled in the smallest part. New forms of inequality and injustice among men and nations such as discrimination, neo-colonialism and exploitation take the upperhand and awaken, especially in the younger generation, a feeling of frustration, hatred and rebellion.

Initially, the thought of using religion for progress and peace in the world seems pointless, for religion, at least in its traditional understanding, is increasingly losing its influence on people. But precisely this disastrous gap between religion and life aggravates the situation. "The alternatives can only be these: to bring about the triumph of a spiritual revival. Religion and life are both elemental forces. Both claim the whole person, all people and human organisations, and this creates the rift between them. The element that they have in common is that they both belong to human nature. True religion is also life and life is also true religion". Since the entire revival has humankind in focus, the archbishop sees an unprecedented challenge for religious people in today's world situation. "Religion has a prophetic role to play in the efforts to help humankind out of the present impasse. It must turn to the conscience of the ordinary man and woman, as well as to public opinion. The demands for justice will either be greatly elevated in the form of war or will be controlled religiously, in the way we, under God's sur-veillance, induce peace. ... The strength of this conference is that it is a meeting-place for the different religious traditions. The question that now remains is whether it will also become a starting-point for a new spirit and a new life-style. Might not one of its results be that we bring all religions so far that they speak unanimously for all people and be the conscience of humankind concerning the burning questions on which depends the survival of the world? Could a summit conference of world religions lead one day to the development of a world authoritative body, to a kind of world parliament of religions, with the independence and impartiality of a court of justice, which would declare, without hesitation or fear, what lay in the interest of all nations …?"

Professor Hideki Yukawa, atomic scientist and Nobel Prize winner for physics, speaks about "a world without weapons" and the efforts of many renowned scientists to prevent an atomic war at any price and thus to prevent any war, since even guerilla warfare carries with it the danger of escalation, and thus also to radically demand disarmament. Here is the greatest rôle for world religions. Until now they have functioned above all for the spiritual welfare of their followers. From now on they must be much more concerned with a better standard of living. "Is the rôle of religion at an end? I believe not. In order to establish an international judicial system which makes war impossible and in order to reach the point where it would be obeyed, friendship, love and mutual trust must span natural barriers and racial differences. The struggle for a world without war cannot be carried on by statesmen and scientists alone. Humankind must take a spiritual step forward and the springboard that we need is love for our fellow human beings — as someone taught us 2000 years ago".

These almost euphorical expectations from the influence of religion on the world were almost brutally destroyed by Professor R. J. Zwi Werblowsky of the Hebrew University, Jerusalem. The fact that the organisers even allowed such a man a hearing proves their courage and realism. The professor believes that the hope of peace of heart could ever bubble over on to political and social structures is a pious wish, but nothing more. The salvation of the world through the change of hearts is an eschatological concept but has nothing to do with social problems. It is not religion with its so-called prophetic function that will change society. On the contrary, socio-economic relations will change religion. "We need to be sensible and remem-

73

ber that until now religious cooperation in the social sphere has scarcely been evident. Neither in the Near East nor in Nigeria, neither in Vietnam nor in Northern Ireland have religious bodies proved themselves capable of working from the inside outwards to disarm religious, racial or political conflict. It is exactly because religious persons, as well as the Churches, do not stand outside society and have a duty to fulfil concerning it, that they are tied up with the economic, social and political interests of their society, despite opposing claims ...". Peace is a political problem, development an economic one and human rights a socio-legal one. Even when a person with religious motives approaches these problems, it does not make the problem of peace less political, that of development less economic or that of human rights less socio-legal. Therefore, we must cultivate the virtue of realism and depend on the experts concerning these questions. "Religious people seem to have to protect themselves against two dangers: against becoming intoxicated by their own words and against over-estimating the meaning of their deeds ...".

This did not hinder Dr E. C. Blake, Secretary-General of the World Council of Churches, after this sensible, but one-sided estimation, from once again examining the relations between religion and development. The validity of a religion must not indeed be judged by its contribution to development. That would amount to a deification of development. Religion, on the other hand, cannot stand in the way of the development process, which attempts to unfold the full human potential as it lies in God's plan. However, development needs the values of a religion to raise the quality of life. Both must mutually support and enrich one another.

There then followed two prophetic calls. The first came from Dr R. D. Abernathy, successor to Dr M. Luther King in the movement for emancipation of the black population of the USA. With stirring words, he addressed all people of good intention and asked, "Why is it that well-meaning people, who constitute the vast majority, have so little influence in today's world? It is because we are timid. The believers of the world have been separated from each other for too long, unsure of their proclamation of the message of peace and reconciliation for all. They have been silent for too long and their silence has been to the disadvantage of humankind. I now maintain that the time of silence is over. Why have believing people been silent? Partly because we have stood alone. Now, however, we are together. But perhaps also because we had lost hope. Silence in hope makes sense but silence without hope works destructively. Silence is a luxury that we should no longer allow ourselves ... . We have met here and have discovered together that God's love, which is the source of all religion, overcomes everything and brings everyone together who earnestly desires the good of humankind. As religious leaders, we must remain together in this non-violent revolution which destroys war, ends poverty and abolishes racial segregation. We must put to one side the comparatively unimportant differences of doctrine. We can have unity without unison, difference without division. We can have a world community without the scourge of racial hatred and oppression, without the sufferings of poverty and without the senselessness of war".

Dom Helder Camara, Archbishop of Olinda Recife in Brazil, spoke in an equally stirring way, "Praise to the Lord for this meeting! A few years ago a gathering like this one would have been unthinkable. We must admit that even today each one of us is aware of the problems he will meet in his own ranks because of this meeting. But, in fact, we have this miracle that the Lord has worked. We are here ... ! We all know very well that humankind has entered a decisive phase and is now capable both of destroying all life on earth and of making it possible for every person to have a standard of living that is worthy of the sons of God ...". He pointed out that religion is a question of development, for it concerns the pivotal question of morality which is to remove the egotism from the heart of individuals and of groups. If the religions stay together over and above all internal differences, they can achieve great things for a new awareness and a new reality in the world.

Hard work was now carried out in the three study-groups, so much so that many sacrificed their hotel meals and sometimes worked through entire nights. As a result, three reports were laid before the plenary council, each one rich in analyses and programmes. Again we select only a few parts, which are directly concerned with the functions of religions.

From the report on disarmament: "We believers admit that the organised religions and their leaders have neither always practised nor understood that religion is essentially linked with all aspects of life, with the political, the social and the economic, and that they have tried to divide life into a spiritual and a material dualism, in which they showed clear disinterest in the material ...". Concerning this, the report on development becomes even clearer: "What should the attitude of religion be towards this reality? First, it should regret being highly indifferent towards the deification of wealth and its misuse. The christian world, in particular, is called upon to regret the fact that (with few exceptions) that part of the world in which wealth is concentrated is the so-called christian part. In contrast to the Spirit of Christ, obstacles have been laid in the way of social justice. The accumulation of wealth has been regarded as a reward for virtue and the burden of poverty as a punishment for sins or as a cross to be born in the hope of release on the other side. After Christianity, other religions must also be criticised since by their emphasis of the relative unimportance of material wealth, they weaken the powers which ought to put development for all into action. The rich person felt safe in his abundance because the masses were encouraged to accept their situation as fate ...". There should be a sound investigation of conscience for all religions! From now on they must commit themselves much more to social justice if they do not wish to counteract the now better-discerned will of God and be dismissed as irrelevant by the people of today, especially by young people.

The western inclination to overestimate quantatives in industry is also definitely rejected. Development cannot be measured by the increase of income-per-head as the Pearson Report suggests. This increase is, of course, necessary but there is still much more in addition. Therefore, much emphasis is put on education for development in order to set up in both the poor and the industrialised nations a hierarchy of values and to make the right motives effective. "We close with the confident statement that the division of the world, due to religious differences, can be overcome and that the unity of the entire human race, proclaimed by all religions to be the ethical ideal, can indeed be realised. This throws a small light into the darkness".

This unity is again stressed in the actual "Conference Declaration", which otherwise has turned out rather lean. "When we were together to deal with the theme of peace, we discovered that the things which unite us are stronger than those which divide us. We find that the following things are common to us all:

(i)   the conviction of a basic unity of the human race, of the equality and dignity of all human beings;

(ii) the sense of the inviolability of the individual and his conscience;

(iii) the sense of value of human society;

(iv) the recognition that power does not give rights and is never absolute;

(v)   the belief that love, sympathy, selflessness and the power of the Spirit are, in the final analysis, stronger than hatred, enmity and self interest;

(vi) the sense of duty to stand on the side of the poor and oppressed;

(vii) the profound hope that good intention will be ultimately victorious.

77

As a result of all these common convictions, we believe that a special task has been given to men and women of all religions to concern themselves, using all powers of spirit and heart, with the achievement of peace and to be servants of peace ...".

There was no shortage of divisions and heated discussions in the study-groups but they developed because of them and turned away from extreme positions in order to find the middle way in the interest of peace.

So as not to quash all ideas and encouragements after the handshakes, the embraces and the bows, a permanent authoritative body was appointed under the title of "World conference of religions for peace". Four programme points were given provisionally:

(i) interreligious seminars and conferences on all levels are to be encouraged in order to create a climate for the peaceful solution of differences of opinion within nations;

(ii) the development of national and regional interreligious peace-committees is to be encouraged;

(iii) the establishment of an interreligious representation at the United Nations and other international organisations in order to guarantee the influence of religion in the solution of conflicts;

(iv) to promote interreligious dialogue for peace in all ways.

Since then all kinds of things have happened. At the headquarters of the United Nations there is the international secretariat under the leadership of Dr H. J. Jack. In Bonn there is an international secretariat under the leadership of Dr M. A. Lücker and in Singapore there is an Asiatic secretariat. In addition, there are many national sections. The second world conference was held at Louvain in 1974 and at present the third world conference is being prepared for September 1979 in New York.[41] Independently of this the "Interreligious peace Colloquium" has been founded in the USA for similar purposes and held its conference from November 7 to 11 in Lisbon.

No one is under the illusion that world peace is ensured by these initiatives. However, it is sensible to have next to the Vatican Secretariat *for* non-Christians an organisation *of* religions where they feel they have completely equal rights and sit at the round table without inhibitions. This has nothing to do with the theological levelling of all religions. Neither can it obscure the profound differences between religions with an evident creed and others with merely a practical ritual or between religions which have freed themselves from any tutelage by the state (even if perhaps only in recent history) and others which are in a certain sense national religions and are not seldom manipulated by political authority. In spite of such and other differences, there is the unity of the religious person that can be no longer diminished. In his religious experience the religious person has many needs and antennae and next to inner peace, the forgiveness of sins and eternal hope, he also wants to take seriously the concerns of world peace today as a religious person. To this extent, such a match is only to be encouraged. Is it impossible to imagine that from these beginnings a kind of "Parliament of Religions" might be set up, which without military divisions could have a moral power? That in the future proclamations such as *Pacem in terris* or *Populorum progressio* would be published by this body and so would have even greater radiating power? Are these merely utopian dreams? It is precisely the task of religions to realise the Utopia of the Sermon on the Mount: to put a new power into the world and to never abandon the individual to resignation and hopelessness.

7

Bishops in Dialogue in Manila

ONE can hardly expect much in the way of new theological insights from episcopal conferences. Bishops are not theological astronauts, who with courage and at risk, fly out into theological outer-space and explore new possibilities. Nor do they simply reiterate traditional statements but try to give new, up-to-date answers to new questions which are posed by the sciences. As a result of their position, bishops are representatives of Church magisterium. As such, they should not, of course, merely hold fast to the old teaching but should also confirm the newly achieved insights of theologians when necessary and thus today also maintain the flow of the development of dogma, as was always the case in history.

If one leafs through reports of earlier episcopal conferences, one gains the impression of a rather introverted Church. The big problems for bishops in old and new countries were the Catholic schools, Catholic press, finances, common pastoral writings, difficulties with the government, etc. Vatican II tore open doors and windows and disclosed the view onto the world. One does not now speak of the Church *and* the world or the Church next to the world but of the Church *of* the world or the Church *for* the world. The Roman episcopal synods, above all those of 1971 on justice in the world and of 1974 on the evangelisation of today's world, contributed something further and sent the national, regional and continental episcopal conferences themes for consideration which suggested new ideas and attitudes to the head of church leadership which would then be worked out in the parish.

The Asiatic episcopal meeting in Manila from November 23 to 29, 1970 must be evaluated in the framework of these considerations. Asia's geographical, historical, cultural, political and religious differences from Japan through Tibet and up to the Near East cannot be painted strikingly enough. And yet, in the post-colonial era, a strong cultural and ecclesiastical awareness of Asian unity is being developed. The biggest continent in the world has every reason to strengthen its self-confidence.

So in those November days, 180 bishops from 15 countries, among them eight Asian cardinals, came to Manila. It was the first completely Asian meeting. It is easy to understand why Manila of all places was chosen as the meeting place. The Philippines is the only Catholic country in Asia. All bishops from the other countries live partly in a choking and discouraging minority-situation. Thus, all feel homesick for Catholic air. For them, to breathe the Filipino air for ten days is like a summer resort, though in 1970 this air was still really stuffy. The people of the Philippines were still the same, constituting an approximate replica of the Latin American Church of the 1950s, before the unrest began which then produced the clarifying programme in Medellin in 1968. Only after the Asiatic episcopal conference in Manila, and partly stimulated by it, did the Church of the Philippines seriously begin its renewal (cf. Chapter 14).

The bishops and cardinals met together for half a week at first. Their main theme (with regard to the Roman synod) was justice and the development of the Asian nations. After regional episcopal conferences had already discussed the theme, they acknowledged for the first time that one should not merely practise charity in small christian communities and serve the rather rich level of society by means of the many schools and hospitals. On the contrary, it is a case of developing the poor people as human beings, to lead them to self-awareness and to inspire them to help themselves. The Church has a function to stimulate all the people; for without justice for all there can be no peace for all. These thoughts were published in a "message".

It must become clear that such a hope could only be realised in cooperation with all people of good intention. Therefore, the bishops accepted three resolutions which are of importance to our context. In Resolution Number 12 they committed themselves "to an open, honest and constant dialogue with our brethren of the other important Asian religions" not only with a view to effective collaboration for development, but with the initial aim "of learning from each other how to become better people". Bishops, who previously represented the teaching and giving Church, suddenly professed mutuality and were prepared to learn afresh and to learn it from those formerly referred to as heathens. In Resolution 13 they assure us that they will do everything so that the life and message of the gospel becomes incarnate in the Asian culture. Only an indigenous Christianity could help in the process of the modernisation and development of Asia to preserve and promote all human values for these cultures. It is, therefore, not a question of folklore, of incarnation into long-overdue forms of religious traditions but into a stirring and self-developing Asia.

Finally, Resolution 14 demands that all associated episcopal conferences adopt the necessary measures to encourage dialogue between the theologians and the experts of religious science of other Asian churches as well as of the Asiatic religions.[42] Ideas which had been started from private initiative and at risk, are now sanctioned and encouraged by the bishops. All deeds of magnitude are accomplished in the Church in this way!

The conclusion and climax of the episcopal conference was the visit of the Holy Father from November 27 to 29. Unlike his coming to Bombay, here he came to a Catholic country — "to his own property". The Filipinos could scarcely believe he was coming until he was there and until they had seen him — hence this massive crowd. There was no shortage of voices in the world press who criticised this visit in advance. How could the Pope prove the honour of his visit to a country and a Church with such a division between rich and poor? Would he risk putting his finger on the wound and denouncing the circumstances?

At the organisation of the programme, the Pope insisted on planning a visit to an extremely poor quarter. The Tondo district was chosen, which the government cleaned up somewhat for this purpose. Anyone who passes through there at a normal time is impressed by the dilapidated houses and huts and also by the crowds of children, who laugh and amuse themselves without toys. They are a happy people as long as they are still children. But the young people and adults feel the misery of life more. Even the Pope can perform no miracles here. He visited the church of St Niño (the Holy Child), a parish of 300,000 people. He encouraged a policy of small steps and expressed his consideration of the worth of all those standing around. "We feel it is our duty, here more than anywhere else, to stand for the recognition of human rights for you and for all poor people in the world". The Church must promote its social and economic emancipation so that they too receive a share of life's prosperity.

At the University of St Thomas he addressed a different-ent group of people: the students, the "present-generation" in whose hands lies the future of the country. 400,000 of them were standing there. The Pope spoke to their hearts. "You are the progressive vanguard of your country. We know of your dynamism. The gospel belongs to you. Do you want to carry it forward, together with all committed Christians, so that you build up a brotherly community on this earth, which the world desires so much?"

Then the Pope was driven out to the newly-built offices of "Radio Veritas". He completed the official opening and used this opportunity and this powerful means to deliver his "message to the nations of Asia". Thus he came out, so to speak, in front of "his house", the Catholic Philippines, and stood, in the Spirit, before the gigantic panorama of Asia. What is Asia to him? What is he to Asia? In today's world with so many secret, common aspirations and so many threatened common values, no one, whether Christian or non-Christian, can any longer pass others by with a shrug of his shoulders.

The Pope began with justified aspirations and then built a "bridge" across the religions. "When we pronounce these exhortations, we are filled with great hope. This hope is not only based on God's help and the responsible cooperation of you all, but also on the knowledge of your virtues and natural characteristics, which are common to you despite all differences from nation to nation. Indeed, when we regard the past history of your nations, we are impressed to the highest degree by the sense of spiritual values which governed the thoughts of your wise men and the life of your great population. The discipline of your ascetics, the deeply religious spirit of your nations, your child-like adherence to the family, your honouring of ancestors — all this points to the primacy of the spirit; all this reveals your unsurpassable search for God, your hunger for the supernatural. May technology not turn you into slaves and may materialism and atheism not endanger you. All God-fearing people of your continent and your religious leaders have to meet this common danger. Asia, where the great world religions were born, should not fall to ungodliness". Then the Pope spoke about the mission of the Church in Asia. "What it has to bring to you, the message of Christ, is not imposed upon you, but is proclaimed in frank and peaceful words. It is offered for instruction and consideration. It will in no way prejudice the cultural and spiritual values of your priceless heritage. In fact, on the strength of its present catholicism, the Church is an enemy of no country or nation. It is bound to make itself indigenous and to assimilate everything of true value. Thus, on the one hand, it will respect the cultural superiority and singularity of each culture and on the other hand, as the Catholic Church, it will convey the values of all these cultures to the others for their own enrichment".[43]

The Pope wisely did not speak here of the "absolute and universal claim of Christianity", a belief that only the believing Christian can accept and which the non-Christian feels is arrogance. He stressed, on the contrary, the "superiority and singularity" of the Asian cultures. And yet from the whole substance, it was brought out clearly that "the message of Christ" has a very special place and the Church of Christ a very special function in the world of religions; and indeed not *merely* as the emporium for particular values to the enrichment of others. It is true that the relationship of dialogue to mission was not intensified here theologically but was formulated charismatically in a tactful and therefore clear way. Manila was worth the journey.

8

Theologians Save the Mission in Nagpur

OBVIOUSLY, the life of the Church, like all life, moves according to the law of the pendulum. All along, theological hotspurs swung too far to the right or to the left and made a point of heresies. This was followed by the backward swing of the Church, which determined the middle way again in a dogmatic formulation. Today we have learnt to give theological pluralism greater room to move and not to cry 'heresy' so quickly. For truth is greater than small minds think. Nevertheless, it can happen that certain accents are put on one side and corresponding corrections are needed.

In past years, dialogue had become the predominant consideration. This also corresponds to the present feeling which no longer thinks exclusively. A desire for the Asian religions developed immediately. People read books about them and believed that they had discovered a true experience of God in them. Thousands of young people flew or hitch-hiked to Asia, to escape western stress and to find humanity and spirituality there. Exponents of church dialogue wander as if mesmerized through the newly-opened gardens of those religions, and not they, it is true, but less enlightened Christians draw from it all the quick conclusion: why then is there still mission? Leave them be as they are. Mission only has the task of making Hindus into better Hindus and Muslims into better Muslims.[44] The radical decrease of vocations in all missionary institutes that followed simultaneously seemed to confirm that the new theology of religions was working in a devastating way and must be stopped.

The previously examined statements from Rome, Bombay, Beirut and Manila have by no means been one-sided. But the emphasis lay, of course, on dialogue. One felt here a great backlog demand. Now, however, it was necessary to report concisely and clearly again what the mission of the Church means today. The 1900th anniversary of Thomas, the apostle of India, who according to old tradition died a martyr in the year 72 in Mylapore near Madras, provided the favourable occasion and a good spiritually historic scene for a congress of theologians on the theme of mission. The men behind the scenes of this conference were the German Fr E. Zeitler, SVD, long-time secretary of the Union of Major Superiors which had stimulated a great deal of discussion among religious institutions, and the Irishman Fr Bede McGregor, OP, from the seminary in Nagpur, which offered its hospitality to the congress.

For men like these, it was clear that mission ought no longer to be understood in isolation, as an alternative, but must be seen as a synthesis in the context of the new theology and of the new Asia. In a continent where Christians are and remain, in fact, a small minority, dialogue can no longer be strangled by mission, but equally mission must not be stabbed by dialogue. In a continent where poverty and other forms of inhuman life are the daily experience of millions and are borne with apathy and fatalism, yet now increasingly provide fuel for revolution, the Church's message of salvation can no longer merely promise the hope of heaven but must turn these harsh realities into salvation. Therefore, traditional ideas about missions must be fittingly renewed. "Missions" were no longer spoken of at all. The uncontaminated, comprehensive and dynamic expression "evangelisation" was chosen and an international conference of theologians concerning evangelisation was called for October 6 to 12, 1971 in Nagpur.[45]

Nagpur is the geographical centre of India and the headquarters for the entire Indian postal service. 93 theologians arrived at St Charles seminary. The majority (70) came from India, of whom 31 were non-Indian, 7 came from other Asian countries, 15 from Europe and one from USA. Once again, it is impossible to repeat the wealth of ideas which were exchanged during these days. One can only try to record the predominant ideas and the new emphases.

In an introductory speech, D. S. Amalorpavadass speaks about the theology of evangelisation in the Asian and Indian context. One must not simply go on principles but also on facts. The problem in present-day Asia is not the preservation of traditional cultural and religious values in themselves, or the acceptance of new, technological possibilities in themselves, but the acceptance of the latter without the sacrifice of the former, or the creation of a new synthesis and a new equilibrium for Asian culture. The Church in Asia is challenged by the masses, who constitute 60% of the world's population; by pluralism, which demands a much more radical incarnation from the Church; by the struggle for emancipation from all forms of neo-colonialism; by the religions, which are rising to new life; by young people, who are extremely committed to and hopeful for a new future; by Marxism, which claims to be the new messiah and by revolution, with or without force. Mission is no longer just mission with churches and catechisms, with schools and hospitals. If the Church gives no reply to all these new challenges, its message becomes irrelevant and meaningless. It has established its lasting existence precisely in giving just the right answer of hope in new situations. Only in this way does it become "the local church" in the full sense, when it goes into the very diverse situations. In the old sense, mission has been a form of triumphal service by the Church, a spiritual attack

88

on the old religions by foreign agents, or, at best, a paternal act by the givers vis-à-vis the "have-nots". The criticism of old missionary methods is developed even further, but then so too is the presentation of what the Church really is and ought to be to make the witness of faith of Thomas, the Lord's disciple, effective in the Asia of today.

Eight studies on the Bible and missionary dynamism were then read out or distributed. S. Lyonnet sees the newness of the gospel in that it sums up the whole law in the one command to love one's neighbour and shows this love as part of the love with which God and Christ love us in the Spirit. Such a message is still very real and valuable today to be proclaimed to all men. K. Luke shows how the concept "witness, give witness" is a basic idea of the New Testament. J. N. M. Wijngaards raises the point that the Holy Spirit himself stood behind the entire missionary witness of the first christian communities and disciples. The experience of the Spirit was the real reason for their own version and the strength of their message. However, this Spirit is still effective in the Church today. Evangelisation is anchored to the very essence of the Church in such a manner that it can never be questioned. The question is only whether we employ human and out-dated methods or whether we evangelise "in the Spirit".

On the basis of all these contributions, it is maintained in the closing speech that Jesus Christ is the source of our faith and mission. The mission of the Church is thus described: "In the Church, Christ goes on proclaiming his message of hope and love to the world. The mission of the Church reaches the ends of the earth and embraces all human expectations and values. Animated by God's Spirit, which knows no barriers or restraints, the Church is called upon to recognise and purify everything that is true and good in the world and in the history of human-kind. As the servant of Christ's cleansing and changing grace, it seeks to bring the whole of creation back to God and awaits the day when all human divisions will be over-come and Christ stands as head of the new humanity which will at last be united and will be filled with his fullness" (n. 7).

Such a definition of mission must immediately remove a mountain of criticisms and previous experiences for non-Christians. Mission remains decidedly "christian". No one can blame us for this. But it has nothing more to do with aggression, controlled activity for the winning of the heathen and the destruction of heathenism. Even the indigenous mission information must be determined by the new view of mission. The function of the builder and the schoolmaster, of the organiser and the administrator can be useful to mission. However, mission itself greatly surmounts this. Today, when all things are questioned, it is a matter of seeing what is decisive and durable. The popular image of the missionary needs certain revision.

After the mission of the Church (behind which stands the guarantee of Christ) is "saved", we pass on to the second theme: the theology of the non-christian religions. The intelligent, modest Professor Y. Congar makes several distinctions and reservations in his text. Because of the uncontested fact that people in those religions can be saved, no conclusions must be made on the value of salvation of those religions themselves. There is no salvation apart from and without Christ. To this extent, Christ and the Church have something unique and absolute about them. Christ is the personal totality of God's plan of salvation. Now, he distinguishes the religions in as much as they are the living practice and experience of their members. In this sense, he admits that the grace and Spirit of God are effective here. To this extent these experiences are means of salvation *by which* those people come to God in faith and love. In contrast to Rahner, Schlette, Cornelius, Thils, etc., therefore, Congar only recognises the subjective aspect of religions while those others, because of humankind's social constitution, point to the religions, as such, as legitimate and desired by God.

Kevin McNamara goes into the delicate question of whether there could be a non-christian revelation. Unexpectedly, he (from the otherwise previously believed conservative Ireland) gives a somewhat nuanced, but nevertheless positive answer. Apart from "natural revelation" through creation, those persons cannot be denied experience of God's love through grace. Such a communication of himself by God is more important than the revelation of a teacher, even if this aspect must not be underestimated in the whole revelation-complex. The speaker does not fail to regard these religions also as carriers of supernaturally revealed truths, but the definite historical attestation as in the Old and New Testament scriptures is lacking here. Nor can the third element be denied that not only individuals but also entire nations experience certain events, victories and defeats as the history of God, and so rightly point out that God is indeed carrying out a kind of teaching process and a salvation-history with them.

Two other theologians, J. Depuis and W. Kaspar, voice their opinions on the question of the salvific value of religions. Basically, both scholars confirm the salvation function but stress clearly the relationship to Christ: individuals are saved not *because* of those religions, but *in* them, *through* Christ. Therefore, Kaspar closes his speech with a clear confession of mission: "Mission is necessary for the sake of the eschatological rule of God among the nations; mission is necessary for the sake of the unity of the nations because this unity is not only a political and an economic problem but just as much a question of reconciliation of hearts; mission is necessary for the sake of the non-christian religions to lead them to a new birth, which they need especially today in order to survive in secularised society; mission is necessary for the sake of vicarious service which we Christians owe to all human beings, especially the poor and the oppressed; mission is necessary as service to the one, redeemed world which is promised to us though the gospel".

Several other speakers confirmed these ideas. In the closing speech the rift between the christian claim and the non-christian religions is overcome in the following way: "India is the cradle of several of the great world-religions. In our days, these religions are alive and active. Christians come increasingly more often into contact with people of other religious traditions. When speaking of these traditions we understand any set of beliefs and practices which represent the human person's ultimate values to which he commits himself in faith and with the hope of finding his final fulfilment through them. The growth of christian consciousness witnessed to by Vatican II leads us to see these traditions in a new light. We see Christ and his grace at work in them" (n. 12) ... . "As there is a universal providence leading each one to his ultimate destiny, and since salvation cannot be reached by one's efforts alone, but requires divine intervention, the self-communication of God is not confined to the judaeo-christian tradition, but extends to the whole of humankind in different ways and degrees with the one divine economy" (n. 14) ... . "Since the human person is a social being, concrete religious traditions provide the usual context in which he strives for his ultimate goal. Therefore, the religious traditions of the world can be regarded as helping him towards the attainment of his salvation. Since those, who are saved, attain their salvation in the context of their religious tradition, the different sacred scriptures and rites of the religious traditions of the world can be in various degrees, expressions of a divine manifestation and can be conducive to salvation. This in no way undermines the uniqueness of the christian economy, to which has been entrusted the decisive word spoken by Christ to the world and the means of salvation instituted by him" (n. 16).

While Bombay 1964 reduced the statements of Küng's, even if in an orderly way, they are now practically confirmed here. Even in a paraphrased form and without using the disputed expression "ways of salvation", it is still asserted that these traditions are ways of salvation, or rather they can be.

These are bold statements from a congress whose main aim was to save mission. Of course, in order to be lucid one adds immediately: "The recognition of the positive relation of the religious traditions of humankind to Christ does not in any way lessen the urgency of the christian mission; rather it is recognised as more meaningful, more human, more universal" (n. 17).

This is further illuminated in the following theme "Evangelisation and Mission". P. Fallon says that in dialogue one needs to speak not merely *about* religion and Christ, but much more. Christ himself speaks through us about justice and peace, about hope and brotherly love, about all true concerns which involve human beings over and above all religious barriers and which have become much more well-known in this time of rapid social change. Such dialogue is not a change of tactics because we stand before an obvious failure of direct evangelisation. On the contrary, it is a sign of greater maturity. The Indian Church has grown up and is entering a new phase in its life in which it stands courageously in the surrounding world and is ready to work together with all the good forces in India. Thus, it is fulfilling its christian service of evangelisation better than it did in the past. For too long it remained isolated and closed upon itself, like a young plant that needs a shady hedge. Now the Church has become big enough and Indian enough to fulfil its valuable christian rôle and mission in India. The yeast has been prepared in the meantime and now it must be mixed with the dough. We Christians did not, at first, have all the answers to all the questions that life poses. In discussion with the others, even we can hear words of christian truth from them and receive rays of christian light and so become better Christians. Only in giving and receiving without any feeling of embarrassment do we come to a partnership and to a christian fulfilment. For this, we must not relate to a common ground but, on the contrary, honour the respective individuality of experiences and achieve a complementarity and mutual enrichment.

While G. Gispert-Sauch discusses similar ideas theologically, A. Fernando continues pragmatically and emphasises that dialogue must not merely be dealt with in intellectual books and be spoken about in élitist meetings. On the contrary, it must be practised in daily life and indeed on the wave-length of today's young generation, which no longer accepts religion in advance as a permanent given quantity, but only considers it to be meaningful if it has something to say in their personal life and for the aspirations of humankind. Thus, he arrives at the theme of freedom, which today is a central issue among young people, but which also turns out to be a basic issue of correctly understood religion. In this view, religion is seen as therapy, an idea which is readily accepted. Christianity is often perceived to be a burden whereas Buddhism leads to freedom, happiness and peace. The "spreading of religion" and "bringing happiness to the people" are seldom looked upon as being synonymous. Yet Buddha and Christ understood it in this way.

A whole series of speeches is again devoted to this subject of freedom *from* or development *to*. Today, salvation can only be still understood as something incarnate, that is promised to the one who now lives and hopes for all his expectations; that also appears as still meaningful in the secular world, since it finds the place of its temporary but nevertheless real fulfilment not outside but in political and social commitment. As Tissa Balasuriya says, in an Asia which has changed more in the last 25 years than in the previous 3 or 4 millennia, one can no longer just proclaim "eternal truths" and write theology in a secluded study. Theology must stand today on the frontiers of life and there make life meaningful.

The commission which prepared the closing speech, not only combined the ideas of the speeches and discussions, but wrote of its own accord, and above all under the influence of R. Panikkar, a splendid text with ten points on meditation in the Church. It was very gladly received by the plenary council and can be described as a typical contribution by the Asian Church. Asia tells the western "manager" Church what the real life of the Church means.

It is reported there very clearly: "In order to be faithful to its mission, a close dependence on the indwelling Spirit is essential for every member of the christian community, since the Church is the presence of the risen Christ at the heart of the universe, renewing and transforming it from within by the power of the Spirit" (n. 38).

... "Only a deep experience of God can give the inner freedom and courage which will make it possible for priests, religious and laity to live a genuinely evangelical life, the lack of which is at present a major obstacle to evangelisation" (n. 43) ... . "In India this is especially necessary if Christians are to enter into a truly fraternal relationship in the Spirit with their fellow-countrymen whose own religious traditions are also profoundly characterised by a sense of interiority and prayer which makes them keenly aware of the immanence of God in themselves and in all things" (n. 44). It is again recommended in a special way that small communities be founded among the ordinary, poor people. "These communities could form centres of initiation into prayer which would be open to the christian laity and the non-Christians" (n. 45). This sacrifice is especially commendable in India where many of the religious communities own monastical palaces. Then, in this spirit, the formation of seminarians and religious is recommended "with special attention to the Indian way of praying". Intensive periods of observation should be made possible even for the people at the front. "A deep contemplative experience will provide a source of inner strength which will enable them to meet difficulties and even failure with faith and serenity. Even if he does not succeed in his work, far from losing his sense of identity, the missionary will find it even more deeply in his union with Christ who achieved the greatest fulfilment possible to man in failure and death" (n. 47).

If we look back on this week of work, we can retain the following impressions:

— Nagpur, in its entire structure and length considerably more important than Bombay, was a true congress of theologians and the first of its kind for Asia. The high degree of western professors at the Asian theological schools was astonishing. They are by no means second-rate people, "good enough for missions". Equally, and even more astonishing was the degree of Asian participants. They are completely conversant with western theology and from this basis they seek to make headway into the Asian truth. The contributions of the Indian world-priest, R. Panikkar, or the Indian Capuchin monk, K. Luke, were, in this respect, exemplary. Participants at the Brussels conference of theologians thought that Nagpur had surpassed that level. We see, therefore, that, in the future, theological congresses must no longer be held only in Brussels or Paris or Rome. Theology has become decentralised. Whereas until now one continent theologised for the others, there are now in all six continents theological colleges, theological journals and theologians who are worthy of this title.

— The issue for future years is precisely the theological encounter of the continents. All have something to give to one another, but have also to learn from each other. Theology should and, indeed, will become pluralistic but it should not grow asunder. They should have knowledge of each other and take the best from each other. Such conferences are in the best sense acts of communion of the fellowship of the Church. Temporarily, the technical knowledge of the western representatives remains quantitatively superior but the Asian republics show themselves to be definitely superior in their dynamism and in their happy confidence. This general feeling stamped the mark on the whole congress.

— The congress reflected a link with the religions but there was no meeting with them. Even when the emphasis lay on mission and not dialogue, the presence of several open-minded non-Christians would have been desirable. Such observers have a most helpful function of control and correction. Indeed, we must be able to express and justify what we believe, not only for ourselves, but also in front of them. We must overcome our fear of such "outsiders". Basically, in the Spirit, they are by no means any longer outsiders to us.

— As a conference on evangelisation, they strived to rescue the main aim of mission. The goal was reached, but quite rightly the two questions of socio-political engagement and dialogue were not excluded, but included. Indeed, both aspects can no longer be separated from the comprehensive term, evangelisation. We know, therefore, that there must be mission, there must be social salvation and there must be dialogue. Whereas dialogue and social salvation can easily be agreed upon, the internal relationship of mission to dialogue still remains problematic. The question, when mission and when dialogue, has not been answered, therefore both attitudes are complementary and not contradictory. The theological and pastoral synthesis of both postulates has not yet become clearly visible enough. To this extent Nagpur I awaits Nagpur II.

9

Liturgical Revolution in Bangalore

BANGALORE was already known as the Rome of India.
However, it might be better called, together with Poona
and Delhi, the motor or the spring-board of India's Church.
For here is situated not its central authority, but its
charismatic section and its "brains-trust"; in other words,
the residents of the many religious houses, different theological schools and above all the national biblical, cate-
chetical and liturgical centre.

Behind this centre there stands the physically slender
but spiritually nimble and tough director, Fr D. S.
Amalorpavadass. He has not only managed to build this
centre with foreign money, but has also given it life (which
is very much harder) and a real function in the service
of the Church in India. For a good ten years, short and
long courses have been regularly organised for lay people,
catechists, nuns, priests and bishops.

Systematically, plans are made and carried out to prepare that minority within the Church which should take
over the leadership and gradually become the majority. No
one who stands by the post-conciliar age and theology can
dispute the fact that the Indian Church needed a change
of direction. It still bore the forceful marks of a static,
clerical, paternal, pious and authoritarian community, of a
self-contained ghetto group, which admittedly owned

well-known schools and hospitals but which remained religiously introverted, like the disciples in the upper-room after Good Friday, "for fear", not of the Jews, but of an over-powerful Hinduism. The stigma of foreign-ness remained with it longer, not only because it had been imported from the West, as opposed to the other religions, but, in fact, also remained in all its forms, in liturgical speech and dress, in statues and pictures, in theology and catechism, in the whole way of thinking and living, a copy of the western Mother Church, from which it was also faithfully born. This must no longer remain the case, for the sake of the Church and for India.

Therefore, at the Bangalore Centre wholly Indian courses were held alongside the usual courses, for example on the ministries, on catechesis and liturgy, at times with published reports reaching 200 to 700 pages. It was a matter of common and earnest basis for research. A climax was the wholly Indian seminar of 1969, prepared by 48 diocesan and 14 regional seminars, which 500 delegates attended to discuss all aspects of church life and to open new ways for the future. Cardinal Gracias acknowledged afterwards: "It has really become a new spring". Others called it "the new Pentecost" or "the watershed of past and future for the Church".

There was also a special study-group there for "dialogue with the non-christian religions". Although some saw it as a betrayal of the old missionary duty, the majority was, however, unanimous that until now a false attitude had been adopted towards these religions and that from now on dialogue with the mature non-christian partners must be built up into the self-understanding of the Church.[46]

This concern, which languished somewhat here in a meeting with many themes, had to be taken up again at the right time. This happened in Nagpur in 1971 and again in Bangalore from December 11 to 17, 1974,[47] but now with a very special aim: people wanted to know the position and function of the holy scriptures of the non-christian religions, what they meant for the Church and whether they could even find application in christian liturgy.

If the celebration of the Eucharist is already the "source and climax of the whole work of evangelisation" (*Presbyterorum ordinis* 5), then it must really become a ceremony and the Church be regarded as an event; it must not merely repeat texts and rites, but give the appropriate space to spontaneity and creative activities; it must also incorporate into the holy event the daily problems, the desire for more dignity, freedom, justice, for fulfilment of the cultural and spiritual inheritance of the nation. Such were the ideas instigated during the first, second and third wholly Indian liturgical seminars held in Bangalore in 1969, 1971 and 1973. A sub-commission had also prepared corresponding models for an Indian anaphora and had put together a choice of texts from the holy scriptures of Hinduism. Both have been used in small groups since then.

However, this could only be the beginning. There was still a huge task ahead. It became clear that, in the future, liturgical texts from Rome must not be merely translated into the Indian languages but interpreted for the Indian culture. There must be an Indian Mass and an Indian hour of prayer quite apart from the fact that, for reasons of foreign exchange, all these expensive books could no longer be bought in Europe in the long-term.[48] After all the preliminary talks, it became necessary to intensify the whole area under question and to examine the experiment for its value.

The task was not made easy. In the previous year, 32 experts (all Indians or employed in India) engaged in the fields of scripture, theology, patrology, liturgy, comparative religious knowledge and philosophy of language composed a work which was sent to all participants for study. They filled a printed report of 527 pages and in their specialisation they represent a still more impressive achievement than the talks in Nagpur.

The seminar itself followed a purely scientific course. As well as the 32 aforementioned experts, there were in addition three archbishops, Mgr P. Rossano from Rome and six secretaries of the diocesan or regional liturgical commissions. Cardinal J. Parecattil, President of the Indian episcopal conference, gave the assembly the impression of Church protection, although he admitted in the opening speech that he felt himself on slippery ground, for because of certain intonations from the press, one sees how the theme comes up against very negative reactions. But then he consolidated himself completely with the matter and said that this study was not a waste of time, but was the necessary preparation for a realistic and successful access to those people who constitute the great mass of India. Whoever thinks that this attitude destroys the purity of the traditional christian values, forgets that what we call christian tradition today has been strongly influenced and penetrated by heathen rites and practices.

They then subdivided into the six scientific areas of interest mentioned above. The bible group asserted (after all we are today better informed about the genesis of the scriptures) that inspiration is no longer understood so much as the quality of one man, the author, but of the whole community and it is indeed no longer the case now that the Bible as such is "inspired" and therefore "holy". It is only letter and "flesh" and only becomes "inspired" when, and to the extent, that it is re-read and re-written in Christ and re-interpreted in the light of christian experience and thus placed under the prophetic word of Christ. This can also apply to books of other religions.

Similarly, the patristic and liturgical group: the decisive point about the writing is not the text itself, but that it is read and experienced by the community as the "word of God". If we accept that the liturgy is the saving presence of the Lord, then the holy scriptures are also placed in this connection. In this liturgical society, the writing is perceived to be the "word of God", but the "seeds of the word" can also be recognised in their most profound sense in the non-biblical writings and experienced as the "word of God".

After two days in the specialist groups, the insights were discussed for three more days in the interdisciplinary group — the full council. In this way, the closing speech gradually matured. In the acceptance that, of course, not everyone would read the 650 page complete report, it was formulated in a rather outline manner which ran to 32 pages. In order to be safe on all sides, it emphasised primarily how they have always remained in contact and in discussion with the hierarchy of the Church both in India and in Rome. Then followed the report on the seminar itself, about this "week of hectic work led by the Holy Spirit" and how the group had arrived at the unanimous view that the non-biblical writings must be incorporated into the life and liturgy of the Church since, in their own way, they manifest the universal salvation which we have received in Christ.

After this, a conclusion of the ideas of the basic papers was given and the newly-posed problem of the non-biblical writings of the Church was immediately pointed out. The old Roman paganism did recognise philosophical writings but not "holy books" like the Asian religions. Now, after the Church in Asia has advanced from an attitude of struggle to one of positive recognition of religions and their functions in God's plan of salvation, it has also been established that their holy scriptures not only help us to discover new aspects of divine mysteries but also to penetrate more deeply the mystery of Christ himself. Thus, the question is posed on the one hand concerning the inspiration of these books and on the other hand about their possible usage in the liturgy.

From the various contributions one can determine again and again that God reveals himself to all of humankind, even if in different ways and to different degrees and indeed not only to individuals but also to groups of people or to nations. In all this the "word of God" is already speaking. However, the holy scriptures are then the "object" of the experience in faith, its institutional expression, manifestation and sign of the activity of God's spirit in them. The revelation in Jesus Christ is not an occurrence that stands alone and isolated, but in him is spoken the last and final "words of God" and the unsurpassable climax of divine revelation is attained. If the "inspiration" of the holy scriptures is taken in its narrow sense of witness and guarantee of the Spirit to his eschatological community in Jesus Christ, then this cannot be affirmed for the non-christian religions; probably, however, in the broader sense as witness of the Spirit, which through the experience of faith and the corresponding writings leads humankind to Christ. In any case, the term "inspiration" allows much analogous application. It is interesting to know that several non-jewish texts such as proverbs, prayers and stories (Ruth and Job) have been incorporated into the Old Testament. Christians are in the position to read non-biblical texts for the first time, to take them from their immediate context and put them into a broader context. Such texts are "the whisper of the word", "original and hidden word of God, but still true divine word". Christ is the principle of the unity of all the Old Testament scriptures, which still did not know *who* he was, but probably suspected *what* he would be. This may also apply to the non-christian scriptures, which according to divine providence, all have a christological and christocentric function. The fact that those religions do not accept this interpretation proves nothing, since even the Jews did not accept the christian interpretation of their writings.

Here it is added that not all theologians shared this particular view of the relationship of Christ with the religions. They are more radical and want to grant those writings and religions their full independence: God wanted them "as such". It is also pointed out that previously western Catholic theologians thought very "provincially" and not in a "catholic" enough way; that they theologised "in blissful ignorance of the other religious traditions besides their own". The encounter with the world religions must now be understood as a sign of the times, which no longer can be overlooked with impunity by any theologian.

Inevitably, this all leads to a great theological pluralism ... .
The uniqueness and individuality of Christ must certainly
not be sacrificed to pluralism.

The explanation of the seminar is now constructed on
this huge foundation. It is stressed, by way of introduction,
that there is no trying to put forward a comprehensive,
abstract solution to the problem, but rather an effort to
seek a flexible and functional approach and to place the
whole within the framework of theological research. "As
members of the believing community of the Church, we
Indian Christians experience Jesus Christ as the Sacrament
of our encounter with God, whom he reveals as the ineffable
mystery that can never be adequately expressed. In our daily
contact with brothers and sisters of other religions, we are
constantly called upon to recognise the striking resonance
of the same ineffable mystery which their religious experience embodies. As we now seek to share our religious life
together, we are brought to a new realisation of the com-
plexities that our faith in Christ is acquiring as well as its
new and astonishing dimensions. For now, more than ever,
we are conscious of a living, mutual relationship with the
experience of the members of other religions" (n. 47).
Then the centrality and singularity of the phenomenon
of Christ are emphasised. With the resurrection of the Lord,
the time has come for the Church to live God's universal
plan of salvation, to make it known and to lead it towards
the eschatological fulfilment. "The religious situation in
India manifests a variety of religious experiences. We
believe that these spring from the action of the Spirit,
in spite of their inadequacies. The Spirit of God is
mysteriously leading all these religions to an ever-growing
realisation of their inter-relationship" (n. 50).

The problem of the non-christian sacred books must
also be seen in this context. For those communities they
are an expression of their ultimate mystery and show the
attested way to the final goal. After emphasising the
position of the holy scriptures in the christian community
it says: "As we Christians grow in our understanding of

the scriptures of other religions, we come to a deeper realisation of their place in the mystery of God's presence among human beings. In the meditative reading of these scriptures in the community, the Holy Spirit leads us to discern his gift which lies hidden in these texts ..."
(n. 55).

Concerning the usage of those non-biblical writings in our liturgy, we can, in the meantime, only tentatively make certain statements and say:

(i) that God has revealed himself in different ways to all nations;

(ii) that their books also deserve respect on our part and such respect is a form of our openness to the Holy Spirit which speaks in them;

(iii) that our anointing through the Holy Spirit helps us to discern the special way in which the same Spirit speaks in those scriptures.

This new dialogic aspect of the Church might find its concrete expression in the way that those scriptures receive a place in the heart of the Church, in the peak of its consciousness, that is, in its liturgy.

The Liturgy of the Word which attunes the community to the Eucharist finds its climax in the readings: the gospel as the proclamation of the good news of Jesus Christ, the other New Testament books as the actualisation of the experience in faith of the apostolic communities, the Old Testament as the historical expectation and promise of our Lord. The experience of God and the expectation of salvation as described in the non-christian scriptures can now be evaluated in this last group. It would open the christian audience to the esteem of those believing fellow human beings and to dialogue with them. The homily as the translation of the writing into the language of the present day would help the audience to overcome the barrier from that expectation of salvation to a saviour, Jesus Christ, and indicate the further anthropological, theological and cosmic connection of the phenomenon of Christ with the non-christian religions. In the way that single prayers and songs from those religions are used at present and individual texts from those books are utilised in the homily, the community could gradually be prepared to accept even the actual reading from those scriptures.

Much emphasis is laid on this pastoral practice. The people must really learn to change their views. They must break out of the sphere of an isolated religious sect. For Christ tore down all separating barriers and proclaimed the community of all believing people. Seen in this way, the leaders of the Church have a hard pastoral task and responsibility, which can only be fulfilled in the openness of the Spirit. The Spirit will lead us out above all fear and uncertainty to a new unfolding of the wonderful life that has been given to us in Christ.

Then the practical counsels are formulated to prevent the whole matter developing into nothing more than sterile controversy. The factual mentality of the Indian local Church must be taken into account. The new ideas must not be forced but must grow gradually in awareness. The hierarchy and the clergy have to assume the leading rôle here. Therefore, in meetings and seminars, they must be theoretically and practically well-versed in those scriptures. Alongside the trial centres which exist already and have been approved by the hierarchy, such centres must be created in every diocese. Those books should be for the time being only used in small groups and paraliturgical festivals. Concerning the choice of texts, naturally only those which do not contradict the mystery of salvation in Christ would be used. The whole thing should also happen in dialogue with other christian Churches. We would, therefore, like to tread really "cleverly" and not rush the matter.

Finally, "a dream and a vision" is outlined as to how the Indian Church in this understanding might look in the future: "The use of Indian scriptures would lead to a radical re-orientation of the Indian Church and so help it to become a unifying force in the pluralism of India's religions and cultures ... . As the human person, to be his true self, must be rooted in his cultures and society, so the Indian Church, to be itself, must be woven into the life of the nation, so that it becomes its "soul" and be able to inspire it with the spirit of Jesus Christ. Indian tradition is enshrined in its sacred books which contain not merely spiritual and religious truth, but an entire outlook, the thought-patterns and accepted values of Indian society. Never can the Church be truly Indian without adopting these treasures" (n. 71).

"An Indian christian community, then, for instance in a village, would live in the style of rural India, share in the fate and struggle of village life, but would breathe the spirit of Jesus Christ in genuine community, sharing and service. It would be bright with hope and trust, would fight for its future with confidence and detachment. Its religious life would move within the patterns of village life, with a daily routine, with feasts and pilgrimages which bring all people together ... . In our cities and industrial centres it would be very different and yet fully woven into Indian life, with a deep concern for the poor, for the untold agony and helplessness of the nameless masses" (n. 72).

Of course, priests, brothers and nuns must go down into such communities, no longer to be administrators but gurus, visible signs of Jesus' presence, the uniting force of the people which reconciles, heals and encourages. Such an Indian community would finally also be the true and effective answer to secularisation, which threatens not only the Church but the whole of India. They close with the statement that, as never before, the great responsibility has been recognised that at this moment rests with the Church, which is led by the Spirit into new and unforseeable ways.

This is the extremely summarised conclusion of this extraordinary week. Among the participants, there also prevailed an extraordinary mood, that of setting-out, as with the disciples when they were sent out into all the world — an "unreasonable" task. One thing was striking at this seminar: the lack of opposition. The outcome could quite definitely be predicted from the beginning. This asserted agreement was even more strange when it was clear to the participants that it was really a case of something quite new in the tradition of the Church and that many circles would oppose it.[49] Certainly, there are in those holy scriptures disturbing texts, but next to them, deeply hidden, are precious stones of fascinating brilliance. Will the Church raise them up and incorporate them into Christ's throne?

The 707 page report emerged quickly from the press in order to give complete information and to avoid misunderstandings, as after Bombay 1964. In the foreword, D. S. Amalorpavadass emphasises that the final word on the question has not been spoken here, but the way to further study and reflection has certainly been prepared. The report desires to be no more than a call to action whilst every decision is ultimately dependent on the authority of the Church. However, he believes that the Indian Church has something to offer in the encounter with the world religions of the whole Church.

The research seminar was at an end and there was anxious waiting and questions. Will the bishops, will Rome itself take the trouble to really read and study the report, to understand the originality of the situation and the challenge, or will they continue in their same old rut and confirm their a-priori attitude? Yet, can they afford simply to ignore this enormous work of the combined intelligentsia of the Indian Church? Months went by and rumours fluttered through the press ... .

One circle that took the report seriously was the international theological journal "Concilium", which dedicated a special issue to it. In his summing up Fr H. Schmidt, professor of liturgy at the Gregorian and at St Anselm in Rome, said that until, and with, Vatican II this question had not been of immediate interest at all. However, no conclusion can be made from this either one way or the other. It is clear that the Old Testament scriptures were never "replaced". However, if good points are found in newly discovered "holy scriptures" of other religions which Christians can relate to Christ and if, therefore, these scriptures receive new light from the Bible and vice versa, then the Bible is enriched by them and theoretically there are no problems in using such books alongside the Bible in the liturgy. This would once again show what constantly has happened in history, namely, that God reveals himself in an increasingly new and more complete way through Jesus in the Holy Spirit on our way to our ultimate end.[50] However, by the time this special edition was published, its intention had already become illusory. For, in the meantime, the long way and the great hope had come to an abrupt end.

Cardinal J. Knox, prefect of the Roman congregation for sacraments and divine worship, sent a letter dated June 14, 1975, protocol number 789/75, to the Indian episcopal conference which does not admonish further study and pastoral intelligence but abruptly declares the whole exercise to be broken off. After two introductory sentences, it reads: "With the intention of guaranteeing the peaceful and harmonious development of liturgical adaptation in India in a peaceful and disciplined way, this congregation respectfully requests that the episcopal conference be concerned with undertaking the following steps:

1) that publications with texts from non-biblical readings for liturgical use be stopped;

2) that the publication and distribution of the "new regulations for Mass" with Indian high prayers be forbidden;

3) that the episcopal conference makes it known publicly that the use of non-biblical readings in the liturgy and the use of the Indian eucharistic high prayer is not allowed, either in ceremonious or private celebration;

4) that every further initiative in this field is first to be discussed with this congregation and no action is to be taken without having previously received the necessary written permission".

The categorical writing ends with the sentence: "I am sure that these measures will help the liturgy really to be a part of Indian Christianity, which has shown so much loyalty towards the Church in the long centuries of its tradition".

This was a hard blow. Certainly thunderstorms prevailed over India's Church and its liturgy and a cool, clarifying rain would have benefited the land. Instead, there came a clap of thunder and lightning that paralysed everything. Questions upon questions are asked in the light of this letter: Why must Rome listen so often to that section of bishops, priests and laity who want to continue to live in the old Church and who only accepted the opening of Vatican II unwillingly or not at all? Why must Rome once again misjudge the novelty of a situation and miss the chance of a breakthrough to the other religions? Must the closing sentence of that letter with the reference to "India's centuries-long loyalty to the Church" not remind us of the fact that up to recent times the Latin Christians in India, out of "loyalty to Rome", led a ghetto-existence, represented a foreign body in the country and contented themselves with an egocentric house-altar devoutness? Must we not think of the tragic end to the Chinese dispute over rites, about which everyone knows today, that inflicted great harm on the Asian Church and that the decision was influenced by theologians in Rome who had no idea about China and only lived for one idea: that the unity of the Church also demanded uniformity?[51] How can this concrete legislation be brought into harmony with the urgent demand for more authenticity and more incarnation of Christianity, as was laid down by the bishops of Asia and Africa at the Synod of Bishops in 1974, and with the new hope which was given by *Evangelii nuntiandi?* How can we believe that we have done enough concerning the matter of incarnation with the well-known "twelve points" (a bow instead of genuflection, oil lamps instead of candles, sitting on the floor instead of on pews ... etc.)? In Rome, 1969, these points were left to the discretion of the bishops

110

of India with the result that now one bishop allows four of them, another eight and only a few allow all twelve. This not only produces new confusion but also creates a new mentality of shopkeeper and casuist. Can it be incontestably maintained that the liturgy must be the same everywhere because it is the answer of the universal Church of God? Is not the liturgy much more the answer of the many local churches, who after all the documents of Vatican II and after *Evangelii nuntiandi* have the right and the duty to be themselves and not merely a copy of a foreign Church and who show the wealth of the one catholic Church exactly because of their diversity? How can it then be that the whole of creation, wherever we glance into a small section, for example, in the realm of orchids, butterflies or seashells, shows an inexhaustible abundance and the Church itself, which consists of creative persons, should follow the same pattern everywhere?

We return to the first question, to that section of bishops, priests and laity which cannot come to terms with the new ideas and has declared much more embittered war on them. In fact the whole question seems to be more of a psychological than a theological nature. Theologically, the whole weight of the Bangalore report cannot just be pushed to one side. And even long before Bangalore, the Dölger-school brought out as much on the influence of "heathenism" on old Christianity. And already in 1958, K. Rahner demanded, as with all matter-of-factness, an impartial proportion "to the observation of religious history, that high culture religions outside Christianity have their holy scriptures. One does not have the impression that our theological works reflected seriously and impartially enough about the inspiration on this fact. However, one did not need to be afraid of the consideration of this homology. A society constitutes itself as historically founded and so it holds out in the light of history into the future almost necessarily by the book. Such a book is consequently an analogy or homology, which is a priori to be expected from the religions which assume a certain culture and under-

111

stand themselves to be the historical religion of revelation. If we add to this that Christianity is the real action of the living God in history in a unique sense (this cardinal assumption is, of course, to be made compared with all religious historical levelling and relativity of the history of religions), then everything else follows by itself and the non-christian homologies become unsuspicious to the holy scriptures of Christianity".[52]

In fact, there are not only too many bishops and priests in India who abide by the traditional line, but also a laity which in a "save-the-faith movement" and in the journal "The Laity" protests vehemently against all flirtations with the heathen religions just as they also protest against priests who go out in civilian dress, who no longer interpret Genesis literally, etc. However, they open their lines for visions of the Virgin Mary in the USA and in Italy, for contacts with the Poor Souls, etc. Why must the Church give way so much to *such* pressure-groups instead of bringing out something about itself in intelligent leadership?

Since that letter, many hopes have been dashed, new initiatives forbidden and theological research blocked. One must start again right from the beginning with great patience and at the same time with great confidence, begin the work with the basis and with the bishops, so that at some time in the distant future the breakthrough into the world of religions will be possible. For this process, much can be learned from Paul, who at the change from the jewish to the heathen church used, on the one hand, the "opposition to his face" against Peter (Gal 2:11) and, on the other hand, in the case of conflict concerning sacrificial meat on the market adopted a much less categorical attitude. He is indeed convinced that this meat bears no further relation to the sacrifice itself and, therefore, is permitted to Christians. However, if others should argue about it, the Christians should abstain out of love (1 Cor 8:7-13). Therefore, he gives the "progressives" right, but exhorts respect from the "conservatives". This is indeed a valid model of opinion.

A recent report states that after three years of shock, certain experiments for a renewed Indian liturgy will be very cautiously allowed again. According to Fides news agency of March 15, 1978, the Indian episcopal conference decided to set up individual liturgical, experimental centres, surrounded, of course, by an entire hedge of safety measures: they must be approved by the Holy See on the recommendation of the episcopal conference; they are supervised by the regional episcopal conference, to which they must submit a report every six months; every year a report concerning the episcopal conference is to be sent to Rome; they must observe all the relevant norms of the Holy See, of the Indian and regional episcopal conference ... .

From the whole issue, it emerges that many church circles have not yet worked on the new aspects of dialogue, nor of social engagement. Above all, they see in them the dangers instead of recognising them as parts of evangelisation itself. On the other hand, the liturgy experiment must not be taken too seriously. More important and more difficult in this most catastrophical land of starvation in the world is the action for justice. Of course, a meaningful, "Indian" liturgy might be given the necessary impulses for this action.

10

Inter-religious Rendez-vous
in Varanasi

EVEN if the fundamental change to an Indian liturgy had been stopped for the moment, the inter-religious encounter proceeded in a dozen ways and in a thousand places throughout Asia, partly in meetings at the highest level and partly in conferences on the basics. Both levels complement each other and need each other. It is completely impossible to survey and describe everything, just as it is equally impossible to be able to specify the type and number of all the flowers in a beautiful field in springtime.

It begins with a completely private dialogue, a kind of Nicodemus-hour, on the street, on the train, in the plane or in temples. Dozens of such encounters were sent to me personally on my reporting journey. Sometimes I mainly contributed to them, at other times I received more than I contributed. The two people always part from each other having seen eye to eye, having discovered each other and having given thanks to God for it.

Towards evening, I embarked from the plane in Varanasi, the holy city on the Ganges, where every year hundreds and thousands of devout pilgrims descend the steps to the river in the profound belief that this filthy water can cleanse them. I was wearing the habit of a

Capuchin monk. I had to wait for several minutes in the lounge for a bus and suddenly a stranger was standing in front of me and surprised me with the question: "Can you show me the way to peace of mind?" If someone is pounced upon in this way on the street in Europe, he would wonder whether that person is lacking in something. To regain my composure I first of all enquired as to who he was: by religion a Hindu and by profession a radio operator at the airport — someone to be taken seriously, therefore. In reply to the further question of how he came to confront me, a stranger, with this matter, he replied, "But it is well-known that such people (in this dress!) have peace of mind".

On the following day I was strolling through the town when someone asked me: "Can you show me the truth?" He, too, was a Hindu, a civil servant in the government. In his hand he was carrying a book of religious aphorisms published by the theosophical society. It was enjoyable but did not satisfy him and for years he had been searching for the truth. I thought I could help him and on a piece of paper wrote the address of "Open Door" in Poona where he could obtain pamphlets about the Catholic religion. The answer was, "I have already read them. I have already read dozens of books. I have had enough of books. I want to meet a man who lives in the Truth". What he was looking for was precisely the Rabbi of the gospels who did not recite theories but invited the disciples to "come and see" (Jn 1:38), to follow him, to live as he lived. I encouraged him with the words "Even we Christians who believe to have the truth, do not see it yet. We are all seekers and believers. One day the time will come when we, you and I, will open our eyes and say 'Ah!'. Meanwhile, however, we have not yet come to this time". Both these occurrences took place in 1961.

In the same year, I was travelling in a train from Bombay to Poona. Sitting opposite me was a modern-dressed Indian. As the train set off, he drew his legs up on to the seat and without a textbook he whispered to himself under his breath. Finally, I permitted myself to ask, "Excuse me, I am a newcomer to this country. May I ask what you were just doing? Were you praying?" With a matter-of-factness he confirmed this, "Every day I recite prayers which I have known and loved for years". At the next station, I asked him to write down one of his prayers for me. While he was doing this, I wrote the "Lord's Prayer" on a piece of paper. His prayer went like this: "God, you are the beginning without beginning, you are the Creator of all things. Everything created comes from you and we are only tools in your hand". As I handed him my paper, I said, "This is a prayer that we Christians like to pray. If you like it, you can add it to your treasury of prayers from now on".

In later years, when I was travelling in civil dress, it was still not difficult to arrive at religious conversation. There they talk about religion just as we talk about the weather. In the plane from Bombay to Goa a Jain explained to me during half an hour how he understood birth, life and death in the light of his religion. I had to admit to myself that really few Christians would do the same so freely and uninhibited. He was a rich businessman.

In the plane from New Delhi to Madras another Hindu businessman was seated next to me. I was interested in his business. After some time I told him that I was a Catholic priest. When he heard this word, he opened his heart to me: "I too went to a Catholic school. But at that time we students were not interested in religion. We only thought about money, a career, success. Now, however, I have reached a point in my life where I can see that money is not the answer. I feel an emptiness inside of me. Each new success and each new pleasure brings back a feeling of frustration". And as helplessly as a child he asked me, "What can I do to overcome this feeling of frustration?" First I replied that this feeling of frustration was already the beginning of grace. It pressures us to look out for final answers. Then I asked him if he had a christian Bible at home. (It is well-known that millions of Hindus

possess at least the New Testament, thanks to the protestant missionaries who took them from house to house.) He
confirmed this. Then I gave him the advice not to read
a page every day, which could become a routine: "But
when you sense that feeling of frustration and await a
word as the meaning of life, then open the New Testament
somewhere, read ten lines and be convinced that through
this old document the living God is saying a word in
your life". His answer was, "I shall begin it this evening".
I do not doubt that he did it and has probably repeated this
experience.

I was in the plane from Madras to Kuala Lumpur. This
time I was predominantly the receiver. A Muslim gave me
a glimpse into his spiritual life: "When I awake in the
morning, my first thoughts are of Allah. Then I wash so
that I can come before him clean. During Ramadan I fast
strictly, but do not find it hard. I think about Allah. I also
like going to Catholic churches. I feel the presence of God
there. Unfortunately not all Muslims still have the same
attitude. My son lives in a muslim student residence but
does not feel happy there. The majority of the students
smoke, drink whisky and laugh at him when he prays.
That is sad ...".

In Bangalore, I visited the famous guru. He started
out by sitting by the road-side. Today he is sought after
from far and wide. With the money sent to him, he not
only maintains his community of monks but has also built
a beautiful temple. While I was speaking to him, men and
women came in, full of awesome reverence. They knelt
down before him, kissed his feet and whispered their
request. He put his hands on their head, gave them a word
of comfort and the blessed went out again overjoyed. All
religions need, and have, men of God who live completely
for God and show men the way to God.

Fr Francis Mahieu, the co-founder of the mountain
monastery Kurisumala in Kerala confessed to me, "I have
already been to hindu monastic communities. I have met
men there who sit all day on a rock, sing a melody to

themselves and pass the day in contemplation. When you meet such people, you instantly change your judgement of Hinduism. You can feel God at work here".

In fact, it is a question of a fascinating discovery. We discover them and they discover us. Why did we have to be divided for so long and "throw stones" at each other from outside?

As well as person-to-person encounters and the big organised congresses, there are also local meetings, which do not cause a sensation and yet work so beneficially. They are sprouting like mushrooms. We shall select just one or two.

On February 24 and 25, 1973, 52 people met together in St Mary's school, Varanasi to hold a "living-together-session". Half of them were Christians, half Hindus, predominantly from Agra, Allahabad and Varanasi.[33] As well as common action on a social, cultural and political level, as well as conferences and study-sessions and as well as common celebration of prayer for all possible occasions a simple gathering for a specific time is the best way to set dialogue into motion.

The participants represented a wide range of every possible occupation and group: Catholic bishops, priests and lay people alongside hindu Sadhus, social workers and students. People of different beliefs mutually edified one another in the holy scriptures, ate at the same table, concerned themselves with the same problems, formed a universal community and felt that the various creeds ultimately have a common basis.

Every morning and evening a celebration of prayer was held. All found it to be the intense time of the day. They all sat in front of an oil-lamp, the symbol of divine light. A hindu Sadhu and a Catholic priest led the celebration together. Texts from the holy scriptures of both religions were recited and heightened in study. All were similarly astonished by the moving of the Spirit in these texts. Psalms and Veda hymns express the same praise, the thanksgiving and the nostalgia. The most uplifting thing was the closing

118

celebration led by a Christian and a Hindu. One could not be distinguished from the other. Both had a hindu name, wore a flowing saffron-vestment, had long hair and a beard and above all, both manifested an equally profound and moving devoutness.

The actual talks had two main points: dialogue and the social engagement of religious men. After a learned lecture about the nature of dialogue, it was said in discussion that we live our life without defining it. This also applies to dialogue. It is clear that dialogue is conversation, exchange and mutual enrichment, the encounter of two partners who respect each other and take each other seriously. It is not argumentation to convince and win over the other. It is established with satisfaction that after the phase of isolation and confrontation, religion has entered the phase of dialogue. Dialogue proceeds from the now accepted fact that God, in his love, shares himself with everyone. But he does this in a rich variety of ways which correspond, on the one hand, to the wealth of cultures, and on the other hand, to the unfathomable richness of his mercy. Basically, dialogue is devotion to God, who is present in and speaks in the dialogue-partner.

On the second theme of social engagement, Professor Parmer said that until now religion had been too occupied with "good works", thus extending the status quo instead of grasping the evil by the roots. He also spoke of the "tyranny of organised religion", which it is up to the religious person to destroy. These statements were somewhat weakened in discussion but not denied.

Swami Sathya Prakesh and Fr Samuel Rayan held a discussion on the question of how religion could become meaningful once again. Religion has a prophetic function to reprimand the world but it must increasingly purify itself and serve selflessly for the salvation of the world.

At the last session, the Bishop of Varanasi, Mgr Patrick D'Souza, secretary of the Indian episcopal conference and warm promoter of dialogue asked, "What should we do now?" The answer came quite spontaneously: "Hold other such assemblies!" Several suggestions for improvement were also brought up: reduce the discussion and therefore devote more time to prayer and meditation; invite not only intellectuals but people of all social classes. The meeting was a certain success. Of course, that does not mean that everything was clear now. In both camps, there still exist considerable differences of opinion concerning salvation, conversion and social engagement. Even a hidden suspicion on the part of the Hindus cannot be denied. One hindu participant remarked, although jokingly, "For you, dialogue consists in your wanting to convert us; for us it consists in not letting ourselves be outmanoeuvred". This statement shows exactly that dialogue is still very important.

Yet another occasion: in the town of Vijayawada in India, the Christians planned to hold a public prayer meeting on Good Friday 1976 together with the Hindus and Muslims. The hindu friends were immediately taken with the idea. There was somewhat greater apprehension concerning the organised Muslims. Fr Domenico Vivenzi, PIME, went personally to the head of the Muslims and cautiously put the matter to him. He had not even finished speaking when the other said, "Father, for centuries we Muslims and Christians have hated each other, fought each other and massacred each other. At last we can gather together and pray, to talk about God and to love each other more. I thank you for this initiative and ensure our full participation". It was, in fact, a complete success and everyone wished to repeat this experience.

Such interreligious meetings have, therefore, become a matter of fact. At the University of Aligarh the "Interfaith society" was founded on the initiative of Archbishop Domenico Athaide of Agra. Prominent Christians, Hindus, Muslims, Sikhs and Jains come together regularly for common prayer and reflection about common questions. Christianity has a catalytic effect here: it unites these other religions not only with the Christians but also among themselves, which previously was completely exceptional.

In order to encourage such meetings and simultaneously to keep them in the realm of responsibility, the dialogue commission of the Indian episcopal conference of 1977 distributed a handbook.[54] Emphasised in the introduction is the fact that it is a matter of a second, improved plan which is, however, still temporary, for dialogue is still developing and growing. There is also no wish to exclude direct evangelisation or the application of justice. Dialogue is only spoken of here as *one* way of christian existence. Not all Christians always have to do the same thing. Each according to the different situations and the various charisms and calls. Then there is information on the various possible forms of meetings, the possibilities and the barriers of participation in worship. For example, one should not enter the temple simply as a tourist, but with the awareness that here also one stands in the presence of the holy reality, without, however, taking an active part in the rites. It is also reported that there are at present in India 13 Ashramas and 15 Catholic and protestant dialogue centres as well as 7 dialogue groups like those of Aligarh in the service of inter-religious dialogue.

11

Francis Visits Friends in Colombo

EACH one of the previously mentioned meetings had set its particular aim on the road towards the other religions: each one strived to stimulate a mutual dialogue, to trace out a mutual path for mission and dialogue, to consider the consequences of dialogue for the liturgy, and to recognise dialogue as a basis for common exchange in the world ... . We now witness two meetings, in which christian and non-christian monks came together to share with each other their experiences in their discovery of God. So, let us begin with a historical model of the dialogue, a model to which we are obliged to be foreign eye-witnesses.

It was in the year 1219. Francis of Assisi had arrived in Egypt in a crusader ship.[55] In the West at that time, the work of christian integration had led towards "Christianitas", towards the city of God in this world, which had established itself as a closed social and religious institution under the sole authority of the Pope and the Emperor. Within this Christendom there was no one who did not profess the christian faith. Heresy was considered as an attempted assassination upon the actual foundations of this society. On every side of the boundaries there lived only the faithless and enemies. Among these were the Saracens who took a particular standpoint as a different socio-religious bloc. The cross and the crescent therefore became symbols of two camps which mutually excluded and opposed each other.

Francis spent some time in the christian camp just in front of Damietta. What he then undertook one day is testified by various chroniclers in such a convincing way that there can be no doubt whatsoever about it. The event caused a sensation at the time and it was because of this that its echo was so widespread. What happened was that Francis stated his intention to visit the Sultan personally and to speak to him about the love of God. All the so-called "wise people" resolutely dissuaded him from doing so. Even Cardinal Pelagius, who had just arrived as a papal legate with an army of reinforcements tried to prevent him from carrying out his intention. In the end he advised him at least to be careful and not to compromise the interests of Christendom. And so, Francis proceeded towards the enemy camp accompanied by Brother Illuminatus, and without any weapons at all. When he was seized by the Sultan's soldiers he declared, "I am a Christian, take me to your master". He spent some weeks in the Sultan's camp. Francis, however, did not consider the Sultan an enemy, but rather an individual, and he was convinced that he too, as every other human being, was really seeking the road to salvation. In fact he did gain the sympathy of the leader. When the Sultan finally released Francis, he gave him a warrant for the whole of his kingdom.

The Christians did not want to believe Francis when he eventually returned and spoke with wonder of the friendliness with which the Sultan had received him and listened to him. In fact he had not been "converted". Francis, however, did not come back to the christian camp with any feelings of having experienced a failure. The visit was significant, not because of its concrete success, but rather because of its great symbolic content: Francis had given christian witness and at the same time had witnessed a brotherly understanding towards those professing a different religion. The Sultan "encountered" him first and foremost as a Christian, not as an enemy but as a friend. Had people learnt by his example, the whole history between Islam and Christianity would have ended up completely different. Instead of talking with one another, people continued to wage war against each other. The breakthrough which Francis had achieved with a prophetic spirit has not been exploited. Only 700 years later are we now taking steps through the opened doors.

The Franciscans today should certainly not see themselves as the only inheritors of this franciscan spirit, which in fact is nothing else but an evangelical spirit. Christ himself used to preach that God in heaven is the Father of all, and therefore his light shines upon all people, and that is why we are all brothers. Everything that took place in the conferences mentioned here in this book corresponds to this basic principle. But the fact that Catholic monks and people of religious orders were allowed to take an interest in the discovery of the Asiatic religions in quite a special way is plain to see. It must fascinate them to get to know the outer forms and personal experiences of so many Asiatic monks. Finally, one can also learn from the enemy, even more so when the enemy starts to become a friend. With this advance into new religious territory, members of religious orders are obliged to carry out a pioneer service, not simply from the selfish point of view, but also for the fulfilment of their prophetic function in the Church.

As a result of all these considerations, a second meeting of the Asian monks' orders was organised from October 14 to 22, 1973 in Bangalore, India; it was led by the Abbot Primate of the Benedictine order, Dom R. W. Weakland. Sixty-one members of the Benedictine, Cistercian and Trappist orders came together, among whom were 19 nuns, plus 30 experts and observers. Amongst the observers were a number of non-christian monks. At the first meeting of the monks' orders of Asia in Bangkok in 1968 people expressed the desire to invite some of the "separated brothers" the next time. This wish had materialised. It is true that these guests did not take the lead, but what they said was important. Already the simple fact of being together opened people's eyes and hearts. In the message which was finally proclaimed to all Catholic communities of monks in Asia, the atmosphere of joy and brotherhood reigned; it was an atmosphere which had been experienced together with the Tibetan Lamas, the buddhist monks, the hindu Swami and Sanyasis. "We have lived together, and we have discovered a mutual enrichment in our common prayer and exchange. We were surprised to assert how in the midst of all the differences of opinion and various experiences, one extraordinary common interest of a basic co-ordination is predominant: to seek God with all one's might. From this common concern there has arisen a very strong bond of unity". The result was that amongst the various fundamental changes, which like Abraham one had to carry out, "we stimulate in a special way the opening to the non-christian brothers, who, as we have already established here, have a lot to give".[56]

What monks and members of religious orders, such as Frs J. Johanns, Jules Monchanin, Dom Le Saux, Francis Acharia, Bede Griffith, Yves Ragain and others have until now as individuals carried out through their meditation centres and their books — often enough amidst complacency or even protest from the Church — is being officially recognised here and now, and is being recommended on a more widespread basis for imitation. This is yet another case which lights up the unknown future of the prophets.

But now let us proceed to that other meeting which one could entitle: Francis visits friends in Colombo. The missionary headquarters of the franciscan order in Bonn which, under the leadership of Fr Andreas Müller, co-ordinated and stimulated missionary activity in 14 provinces with 1600 missionaries (in Germany, Austria, Holland, Brazil and Indonesia), has already carried out 10 international seminars for the confrères in Europe, America and Asia, the cost of which was borne to a large extent by the Friedrich-Ebert-Foundation. The tenth seminar took place in Colombo, Sri Lanka, from November 13 to 18, 1977.[57] This seminar brought together 20 franciscan monks from Pakistan, India, Sri Lanka, Indonesia, Korea, the Philippines, Hong Kong and Japan. The sheer event of a convention of such a mixture of brothers is something valuable, and it is an experience which one would not like to miss out on. In this closed company also sat a few representatives of the non-christian religions. The theme was dialogue with the Asian religions as a prerequisite for the entire human development. This has seemingly nothing to do with Francis of Assisi. And yet, whenever he was spoken about, even when very little was said about him, the whole atmosphere echoed his spirit: the involvement with one's neighbour, religious discussions with him, solidarity with the poor, the concern to help people increase their insight into their dignity as children of God. These existential franciscan values were raised by Bishop Paternus Geise, at present Rector of the Catholic University, Bandung. At the time of the confrontation in the famous meeting with the Sultan, Francis sought understanding and compromise. He replaced force with love, and in this way he opened the way to peaceful co-existence.

Professor A. Camps from Nimwegan, the President of the international and interconfessional Union of Missionary Studies, made the opening speech. He led different experts in saying that the awareness of development as a dynamic, compelling force was the most important element for actual development itself, but that the religions themselves were keyed primarily to statistics, tradition, upholding of the existing order, acceptance of "the will of God" and respect for the world. He said that as long as this type of religious attitude did not change, one could not hope for a true development, since the religious person wanted to be motivated in his actions in a truly religious way. Therefore, Camps concluded, religion had to be interpreted in a different light, and the moving forces within religion towards a development had to be discovered. Just as we had made great progress in Christianity in this aspect,

126

and had found our motives which have helped to stimulate development precisely in the belief in the Creator, so too we had to help the Asian religions to become religions which were well disposed towards progress. If the religions did not yield this motivation towards development, the atheist ideology of Marxism would come and force its own development. This was a question of the future of the people and the future of religion. We could not abandon people to Marxism, which — if not already — satisfied only the economical and horizontal claims of the individual, and not the vertical and unlimited ones. Churches nowadays did not emphasise as much the quantitative aim to increase their number, but rather the qualitative aim; as a result the followers practised the function of fermentation so that they could change the atmosphere of life, and give people new hope and renewed confidence in their surroundings.

In three lectures it was then shown how these questions stood in concrete terms with regards to Buddhism, Hinduism and Islam. From these lectures it was inherently evident that any development could not only be a question of increased production and economic growth, but it had first and foremost to be a question of changing the individual as such, together with his spiritual values. If there were an alternative, one would rather pass by, forsaking the Asian person in his patience, satisfaction and devotion amidst the poverty, rather than delivering him to the stress of the western world and to the unsatisfying rat-race for wealth and pleasure. Neither technology nor a hedonistic understanding of life were true ways; only the whole-hearted development of the individual in all his dimensions was of any value.

What stood out amongst other things in the study groups was that at that time, Francis had a warm reception by the Sultan because he was an unpretentious poor man, whilst nowadays the Church appeared to be far too rich, too powerful and too organised, and therefore this always provoked a certain uneasiness and suspicion between people in discussion. The franciscan attitude was for that reason so necessary, and could provide a feasible alternative to the threat of Communism. It was not in vain that Francis was highly esteemed in every Asian country with his love for everyone, with his endless devotion to the Father in heaven, and with his joy in the Creation.

An effort was made to communicate to all brothers in Asia what had been seen and learnt here in one final report. It was pointed out: "Dialogue with the Asian religions as a prerequisite for the entire human development means to search and to find the common human and religious values in the different Asian religions. Such a dialogue is a dialectic process of giving and receiving, based on mutual respect and esteem of values. With this attitude we are searching for the maieutic approach towards dialogue, in other words, we are trying to discover within these religions themselves the value systems which possess these qualities for salvation. The first inference of this opinion is that we do not force upon them from the outside our own value systems. We shall not, therefore, push Christianity and the jewish-christian values onto Asia as something foreign, but rather we are seeking much more in the Asian experience the same ground, which makes it possible in dialogue to accept our values as the fulfilment of their deepest hopes ... . In this sense we shall first be able to find out the motives for development within these religions. Should such motives not be forthcoming, then development would be doomed to failure before it even started, because it would only be imposed from outside and would not correspond to a deep-seated need. This is what has happened in so many development projects, where a foreign technology, based upon a foreign judgement of the individual and the world, was imported ...".

Then it was shown how Buddhism chose silence and loneliness as the path towards freedom and self-realisation against the suffering and the evil in the world, whereas Christianity tried to concentrate more on destroying the roots of evil by a positive alternative and by building up God's kingdom here and now. Hinduism likewise harkened to nature and God's almighty presence with great respect, and came into a deep communion with it, whereas Christianity, on the other hand, sought more to master the world and to achieve economic and scientific progress. Finally, in the islamic faith, above everything else, God, the almighty and all-compassionate, was sought and revered, whilst in Christianity a person was seen as a responsible fellow creator. In each of the three cases the two respectively different viewpoints are complementary, and a lot can be learnt from them.

This whole way of speaking and this basic viewpoint is already of a very franciscan nature. At the end it was explicitly emphasised how Francis, a man who really lived the faith in Jesus Christ, would be an everlasting model for dialogue. To the Buddhists he appeared as an example of unselfishness, empty of his own desires, but open for the Absolute, the king of Creation, not in the sense of possessions, but in the sense of love towards every creator. The Hindus saw him more than anything as the author who did not draw scientific conclusions, but who through enlightenment saw things in their right light and who went his own way. The Muslims always considered him as a pioneer of dialogue and of humanitarian encounters, which opened the way to peace in the world. "Francis was able to be so wonderful and defenceless because he had nothing to lose. He had previously given away everything and had set his whole trust in God. In this way he will always remain for us a source of inspiration to seek true dialogue between Christians and Muslims".

One should not forget that Wednesday afternoon, when the whole group visited four religious shrines, a buddhist monastery, a hindu temple, a mosque and the baroque Catholic cathedral, where everywhere was abounding in contacts and conversations which were valuable, and yet which at the same time showed that there was still a long way to go from the worthy theory of dialogue to the actual practice of it, and that not all Franciscans were Francis and not all Muslims were the Sultan.

At the end of the seminar everybody felt that they were at square one, that the way towards common development was more like a difficult mountain walk rather than a pleasant stroll; they felt that above all it was far easier to talk about Francis and to rejoice in his sympathy of Asia than to live like Francis and to put into reality the Utopia of the Sermon on the Mount in a particular place. And yet it had become clear to everyone that the franciscan evangelical life could be a possible answer for the challenge of the time, a path in a future worthy of human beings.

Discussions Between Muslims and Christians in Indonesia

BY looking at the Indonesian school atlases it becomes clear how important Indonesia considers itself to be. One is led to believe that the globe can be spun in such a way that the 500km-long island kingdom comes to rest in the middle of the map of the world, flanked by Asia, Africa and Europe on the left, on the right by the two Americas, and below by Australia. The Javanese like to call their country "pusat dunia", the centre, or to be more exact, the cornerstone of the world. That may all be somewhat excessive, but nevertheless, after China, India, Russia and the USA, Indonesia with its 140 millions is the fifth largest nation in the world. Its roots stretch way back into the mists of time for it is here that traces of "homo erectus", human-like beings are to be found, dating from around half a million years ago. Negroids and Australoids have also been in existence there for almost 30,000 years.[58]

As far as religion is concerned, Indonesia is the largest islamic nation in the world. There is in fact a lot of controversy over the exact statistics. Politicians like to talk about 130 million muslim Indonesians, or as a percentage: 95% or at least 85% of the population. However, real figures show that only 50 to 70 million official Muslims can be counted, and furthermore that their islamic religion should not be compared with that of the Arab states. It can be said that Islam changes in proportion to the distance from Arabia, through India, until it reaches Indonesia, in the sense that there is a greater liberalisation and a mingling of several pre-islamic religious elements.

If this above calculation is correct, in addition to about 10 million Hindus and Buddhists and roughly the same number of Christians there remain 50 to 70 million ' others"; that is Animists, followers of the original religion, that is to say the pre-hindu, pre-islamic, pre-christian religion. They are often simply counted as Muslims because they bear an islamic name and because since the time of Dutch colonialism all non-hindu and non-christian marriages have had to be contracted in a mosque, which has therefore led to false calculations whereby all these people have been counted as Muslims. From these ranks of "others" Christians have been recruited and have also recruited.

In 1977 Catholics numbered about 3.5 million, while there were more than double this number of Protestants. Indonesia, therefore, has more Catholics and more Christians than any other country in Asia, except the Philippines and India. However, on a percentage basis, whilst 1.5% of the Indian population is Catholic, in Indonesia the ratio is 2.1%.

Figures do not count for much. It is the effects which are important. In this respect, in many Asian countries, but to quite a special degree in Indonesia, the public influence of Christianity is proportionately opposite to its numerical size. Through the schools and hospitals, the Church, above all the Catholic Church, represents a conscious element in the life of the people. The Indonesian, A. Abimantrono, said in a speech that "since the last century the Catholic Church in Indonesia has controlled the whole educational system through the schools and has in this way created a neutral and sympathetic 'breeding ground' for mission". The non-christian civil servants fight to win a place for their sons and daughters in christian schools. In this way the Church is able to influence the officials and to protect its interests.

A further example of the Church's powerful influence is *Kompass*, the most important daily newspaper in Indonesia, with a circulation of 270,000. Every morning it is flown to the 30 largest cities in the country. Without being a "catholic" newspaper the investors and all those behind it are nonetheless Catholics. However, on the whole it is a political, economic and cultural journal which tries to convey objective information in an unoffensive way whilst upholding universal moral values. 54% of the readers are university graduates, 48% are Muslims. Considering that on average one newspaper is read by at least three readers it becomes apparent that the *Kompass* has a big impact on the moulding of public opinion. Now, however, we come to the crux of the matter: the relationship between the islamic majority state and the christian Churches. Compared with the "Cinderella" existence of Christians in other muslim countries there is no doubt that the Indonesian Church holds a privileged position. It enjoys not only complete religious and educational freedom but the state also regularly invites religious discussions on national radio for civil servants and military troops with the result that the Church cannot fully exploit the available opportunities.

On the one hand, this friendly relationship stems from the history of the National Revolution which began in central Java, where the Catholics were relatively strong and joined in right from the start. There existed at that time, and still exists today, a very warm and friendly rapport between many leading Muslims and christian laymen or bishops. On the other hand, these cordial relations are supported by President Sukarno and his successor Suharto's state philosophy which is an openly religious format. This philosophy, the "Pancasila", is made up of five pillars. It states:

1) belief in an almighty God;
2) an impartial and developed humanism;
3) the nationalism and unity of Indonesia;

4) an enlightened democracy;

5) social justice.

These principles are considered as absolutely sacred. "A man without religion is not considered to be an Indonesian, not even a normal human being", President Suharto once said in a speech. At the same time religion is looked upon as a bastion against Communism. A positive tolerance is therefore practised towards all religions. Nothing is more frowned upon than religious tension and arguments. An islamic state of this kind would indeed seem to be an example worth following.

However, all that glitters is not gold. Despite the official government viewpoint, in practice, as so often happens, there is much which gives rise to criticism and discontent. Church circles point out that the government favours the Muslims to an unwarranted extent. It is true that they also pay the Catholic religious teachers and present Catholic missions with the Bible but that bears no comparison with what they do for the muslim religious teachers. Moreover the islamic structure of religion is being eaten away by corruption and it seems impossible for anyone to lift a finger against this. One statistic says that in 1973/74 eleven ministries had a combined budget of 15 thousand million rupees, but the Ministry of Religion alone had a larger amount at its disposal so that it could help islamic circles with the building of mosques, wages, pilgrimages to Mecca and with money which simply disappeared into pockets, embezzled by government ministers down to heads of villages.

In spite of this, islamic circles are not happy with the situation. The right wing have always wanted Indonesia to be declared an islamic state with all the consequences of such a totalitarian theocratic system. They feel frustrated because this has not yet been achieved. They also have a deep-seated fear of the influence of Christianity and speak openly of an overwhelming "christianisation" of Indonesia. It is widely reported that if no action is taken, then

Indonesia will be christian in 25-50 years time. From time to time smear campaigns are waged against the Christians and it even comes to acts of violence. If, besides this, Jehovah's Witnesses or similar groups are also active and their members carry out intrusive house visits, it is no wonder that the muslim leaders see red. In their communiqué at the end of their 1975 conference, the Catholic bishops particularly stressed that such groups had nothing to do with the official Church and that their practices were not in keeping with the true christian spirit. In spite of this, the Church is seen as an advance party of the world power of Catholicism which with strong discipline and well-aimed funds is steadily increasing its sphere of influence. Even the developmental aid of the western world is seen in this light as disguised, but nevertheless significant, efforts to build up the West's (or in other words: Christianity's) influence. The former Prime Minister, Mohammad Nafsir, wrote: "It is naïve and extremely stupid to pretend that foreign mission organisations with their unlimited capital and specialists in religious, technical and scientific fields came exclusively to Indonesia to assist in the raising of the living standard and technical knowhow of the Indonesian people. Indonesia is the object of a christianisation from all sides of the world". He urges the Christians to live in respect and tolerance and not to use their resources for proselyte meddlings.

Rather than sounding the alarm about the strength of Christians it would be better to exert oneself for the development of the country. However, therein lies the weakness of the traditional islamic masses and their poorly-educated leaders. They are renowned for their fanaticism and corruption but not for their expedience in the construction of a modern state. Today's youth therefore rejects this religion. Progress is required, and that particularly in a land which, because of its products and mineral resources, could become a wealthy country but whose per-capita income in 1976 was only just over 100 dollars.

A further reason for the tension is produced by the

ethnic contrasts. The christian Batak from north Sumatra are looked upon as superior. In government and trade everywhere they push their way to the top and spark off corresponding bad feeling. In the same way, there exists a political-religious tension between the Dayak, who are becoming christian, and the muslim-Malaya in Kalimantan. For that reason nearly all Dayaks declare themselves as Christians in the census and thus suddenly number 100% to 350% more than in the parish registers. How can one escape the dilemma of the strong and yet so fearful Islam and the weak and yet so strong Christianity?

Already since the 1960s talks have been repeatedly held between the Christians and the Muslims and indeed have been backed by the government itself, thus in Bogor in 1961, in Jogjakarta in 1965, in Jakarta, Bandung and Malang in 1967. A leading figure in these talks was Dr Mukti Ali, Professor of Religious Knowledge in Jogjakarta. Much more emphasis was placed on the need for tolerant co-existence and much less placed on theological and spiritual questions. The discussion hinged on "Dialogue in Action". The same Dr Mukti Ali was also present in Ajaltoun-Beirut in 1970 where he gave a talk.[59] He began with the Day of Peace which had been called by Pope Paul VI and wondered why peace was always only an ideal and not a reality. An honest self-appraisal and an admission of one's own shortcomings and faults was needed from every state and above all from all religious communities. Indonesia was an islamic country enjoying good relations with other religions. Nevertheless there were more and more tensions because the conduct of the Christians was offensive in the eyes of the Muslims. The Prophets and the Koran were spoken of in an insulting manner, and people did not shy from lies and slander. Furthermore, he accused the Christians of building their big triumphant churches in areas which were completely muslim and flaunting their money from the West whilst the people of that area scarcely had their sufficient portion of rice for the day. In 1967 the President had wanted to suggest to both sides

136

that missionary activity should be dispensed with. However, the Christians did not take up the suggestion. Thus after that, the Muslims were the object of their mission. A genuine dialogue failed to materialise because the Christians put the Muslims and the heathens on the same level. Their plan for Christianisation was nothing short of pathological. "Peace and justice can only be upheld if there is cooperation instead of competition, fraternity instead of animosity, trust instead of prejudice. What concerns the Muslims is that their hands are continually outstretched to their christian brothers. They believe that we are no longer in the Middle Ages, when the spirit of the Crusades prevailed ...". This rather one-sided show was somewhat out of place in Ajaltoun. It did however point out that we must be a bit more careful with our powerful presence in Indonesia.

In 1971, Dr Mukti Ali became Minister of Education. In this office he organised a whole new series of official talks. His learning and knowledge never failed to astound. Some said that he knew the Catholic texts better than the bishops. However, one increasingly gained the impression that at heart he still remained a narrow-minded Muslim. He embarked on different ventures in the interests of Islam and also did not sufficiently check the corruption in his Ministry. Thus at the Indonesian People's Congress in 1978, he was dismissed together with eight other Ministers.

This People's Congress from March 11 to 23, 1978 was looked upon as a political and religious event of the greatest importance.[60] The country had been making considerable progress for some years already. It was able to support its own currency, develop the road network, increase the number of schools and realise irrigation projects. Action had also been taken against corruption, and a fair number of business men and government officials had been exposed. Furthermore, the firm declaration had been made that the 10,000 political prisoners imprisoned before 1979 should be set free, if they were not going to be formally sentenced

137

by a court. In conclusion, the general election of May 1977 showed a clear support of government policy. That was altogether a good starting point for the People's Congress which takes place every five years and was attended this time by nearly 1000 people.

Whilst preparations for this were being made, the fanatical Muslims had again dominated the streets and spread their propaganda. However the tolerant and progressive group clearly had the upper hand in the Congress itself. One of the main themes was the question of religious-mystical movements (Kebatinan) which rest on the foundations of the pre-islamic and pre-hindu cultures and cultivate a kind of cosmic religion which for years has increasingly made itself more and more apparent. Before that time they had simply been counted as Muslims following the well-known "remainder theory". At this People's Congress they received official recognition of their status in relation to Islam, Hinduism, Buddhism and Christianity. They were allowed to organise their own schools and receive support from the state. They were also officially granted a position amongst the "Believers in an almighty God" so that in the spirit of the Pancasila they enjoy full equality of status. President Suharto's opening speech clearly followed these lines of openness and tolerance. At the end he mentioned that by the grace of God the Almighty, only three weeks before he had opened the majestic and beautiful new Istiqlah Mosque in the capital. This mosque was the pride not only of all Muslims but also of the citizens of Indonesia. "It stands side by side with the beautiful Catholic Cathedral. Let us then accept this fact as a symbol of the harmony between the followers of the different religions in our state, which is founded on the Pancasila".

Thus Indonesia continues on its way into a brighter future. The new cabinet is made up of 11 generals and 14 technocrats: prestigious men who have studied in Germany, France and the USA, a kind of technosophic-bulldozer type who have a deep faith, but who do not consider religion as the cause of tension but regard it more as unity, not as an obstacle to progress but as a stimulus. They see in this the specifically Indonesian identity, that all religions have the same right, that all forces and elements, even foreign cultures should be welcomed in the country providing they only enrich the Indonesian culture.

When one questions Eurocommunism and asks oneself whether within the marxist system a true pluralism is really possible, here in Indonesia, it has become apparent that within Islam a true pluralism has become reality because of the state's political realism and also because of the theological contemplation of the equal value of all human beings and their freedom in religious matters.

Those familiar with the situation can now see some good years ahead, but suspect that the most difficult situation since the Declaration of Independence in 1945 could come at the end of the present five-year period. Until now there have still been a few "heroes from the early days" in the government. They held the people together and lent a certain prestige and charisma to the government. This generation is now dying out. Will the young leading class continue along the same lines? History never gives an advance guarantee. That makes it interesting and exciting. The verdict as to whether a generation has made full use or not of its time and opportunities is always only clear in retrospect.

From the spirit of evangelism and an interest in the Indonesian people have arisen some stipulations for the Churches who have been accepted as partners in the building of the nation. They should perhaps practise the spirit of kenosis a bit more consciously. They should not misuse their privileged position in the schools and hospitals, nor exploit it at all to create advantages for the Christians. Such operations are no longer ways of propagating the gospel, but rather unselfish service to the people. Moreover, all of us are interested in a better education for the Muslims as such. Through the contact in the schools, the prejudice and underlying mistrust towards us can be broken down so that the Muslims overcome fanaticism and arrive at a purposeful reality through a better education.

At the same time, the spirit of the argument is important. The Church should be the self-examining conscience of the state and should not happily give up its activities in the shadow of the state. The negative side of the good relationship with the government lies in the fact that one usually shuts one's eyes, for example in the question of corruption and political prisoners, and therefore holds joint responsibility. Silence is consent. Alas, when a country lacks prophets who, if not the Church, will have the courage to point out wisely and yet clearly conditions which are unjust? It has happened in a few cases. In 1974, 41 priests from Jogjakarta wrote an open letter against some corrupt officials. They actually received more expressions of support from the local and national press than from their own circles! In 1976, in connection with the Soweto affair, a collective petition against corruption was signed by the President of the four religions and also by the representative of the Catholic Church, Cardinal Darmojuwono. These are isolated incidences. We know from experience that where the churches in Latin America, the Philippines, etc. rose united to the defence of human rights and voiced everyone's opinions, they have had nothing but success. They have become symbols of hope for the people and for themselves, for only this kind of religion is taken seriously and will survive.

Until now the Church in Indonesia has remained very western-orientated, for example in theology, liturgy and church music. Its high level of achievement in schools and hospitals can likewise be read as a typical sign of western management, while the spiritual side has not developed in the same way. For years a conscious effort has been made in India to stress and live out the spiritual values in Ashramas and in a religious-mythic dialogue with other religions. In Indonesia we are awaiting this kind of wave. Most people became caught up in the operation. The Trappist Abbey Rawa Seneng is a happy exception. It has become the centre of spirituality and is open to both Catholic and non-Catholic visitors. Quite a few decide to stay for some months or years. Charismatic groups and other basic communities should be encouraged to break-up the large anonymous parishes and to establish the Church as an experienced community. In Java, quite a few Catholics go to church on Sunday but during the week they have to go to the meetings of the Kebatinan. They therefore feel the need for more fellowship and a deeper experience of God. If we do not offer it to them they will seek it elsewhere, and they are quite right in doing so. This is a case which illustrates how we are challenged by other religions and how in our relations with them we can become better Christians.

13

The Interpretation of the Chinese Experiment in Louvain

DIALOGUE amongst religions is both good and right. The demarcation-line which divided the world into christian and non-christian, thus creating two virtual enemy camps, had to be crossed in the end. Yet a second demarcation-line exists, separating people into believers and those who succumb to an ideology. Instead of mutual animosity can there also be dialogue here? Certainly, since demarcation-lines are never a final solution. They are always being infringed upon, crossed and removed. The human person is always attracted instinctively to bridge the gulf between differences, to overcome disparities and to bring the pendulum swing between the thesis and antithesis to rest at the synthesis.

When speaking about ideologies (by this we mean people's convictions which are only allegedly governed by realistic principles, but which are in fact governed by the aim of fulfilling subjective interests), we are not thinking solely about marxist countries. There is also the ideology of "progress without frontiers", of the "American way of life", of liberal capitalism. There is the rightist marxist dictators' ideology of "national security", the ideology of the "select few", which is expressed in exclusiveness and apartheid. Finally, the marxist ideology, which itself becomes a dogmatic pseudo-religion within the whole religious struggle. All these and other ideologies exist not only outside, but also within the confines of the Church. Dialogue between ideologies is therefore not only a question for the Church's exterior policy, but also for its internal policy. As far as possible, tensions and conflicts on both these fronts must be defused.

For the past 10 years the World Council of Churches has had a "Secretariat for Dialogue with Ideologies and Living Beliefs". The Vatican is seeking to accomplish this task by means of two separate secretariats, one for "non-Christians" and the other for "non-believers", which means that the second secretariat is by no means as dogmatic as the first. This is also due to the more difficult task.

Now let us turn to the most significant and fascinating case of ideological discussion: China's experiment. At present Russia certainly has more influence as a political and military power. She is both ready and in a position to support her partners to the end and to offer effective military aid, as was the case in Vietnam, Angola, Ethiopia, and as is shortly to be expected in the southern triangle of Africa. But such massive aid does not produce friendship, but rather dependency, fear and resistance. Two such unequal partners can hardly remain on good terms for any length of time. It can be foreseen that the African states will need Russia. As a result of African nationalism and Russia's psychological clumsiness, the African states will seek to shake off this friendship again when they have achieved their goals with Russia's help.

In this respect China has more tact. When the Afro-Asian states joined the United Nations, with a vicious shout China's representative, Chiao Kuan-hua, explained that China did not see herself as becoming a third world power alongside the USSR and the USA. She wanted to be small with the smaller powers in order to work with them to thwart the superiority of the super-powers. China saw the great reality of the future world in the new self-awareness of the nations of the Third World. In the long run, he said, China would have more friends and influence in the Third World than Russia and America because she too could put herself forward as an historical model of how a very poor country could overcome its underdevelopment through its own means within a relatively short time. Etienne Balazs could have been quite right when he stated as early as 1954, "the twenty-first century of the Chinese will follow our century of the Russians and Americans".

Whatever one may like to think about China, it cannot be denied that in thirty years the largest nation in the world has been lifted out of hunger, disease, ignorance, epidemics and floods. Through enormous effort the rivers have been dammed, the 1.3 million "barefoot doctors" have extended a health service throughout the country, children are guaranteed an education and the young people are guaranteed a job. The standard of living is nowhere near that of the West, but life is so much better than it used to be. We know what price had to be paid for this experiment, and another nation would not begrudge China the brutal removal of hundreds of thousands, or possibly even millions of "counter-revolutionaries", and the strict limitations placed on religious and human freedom.

It seems that the present régime under the leadership of Hua Kuo-feng intends to proceed on a more liberal and pragmatic basis and wants to grant the people more freedom and pleasure. This has always been expected. For the Chinese are too intelligent not to realise that the human person is only happy when he is free, and that as a result of the crisis period and the hardships of the first three decades, somehow the hold on the reins had to be relinquished. In Hong Kong in November 1977, I was in fact told that nowadays approximately one million Chinese a year move legally to and fro across the border, and also that postal traffic functions normally and that intellectuals are again free to speak their thoughts.[61] The Chinese are living in the euphoria that in 20 years' time China will be the leading nation of the world.

As the situation continues, Christians can no longer

simply ignore or boycott and criticise the Chinese experiment with malicious joy. On the contrary, when we interpret history as a whole as being salvation history, we must ask ourselves: how should we see the Chinese phenomenon as a sign of the times? What is God wanting to tell us by the fact that within 30 years 800 million insignificant people have achieved dignity and international significance? Could it be that the human power which lies behind such an event is latent christian virtue which is recommending us to follow suit in order that the face of the earth be renewed?

Such questions drove the leaders of the Catholic socioreligious research bureau "Pro Mundi Vita" in Brussels and of the World Confederation of Lutherans to invite specialists in both confessions to discussions which took place in Louvain between September 14 and 19, 1974.[62] For more than a year preparations had been carried out and contacts had been made with individuals and groups who were working on the analysis of China. A preparatory meeting with 22 participants was held in January 1974 in Bastad, Sweden. Here 17 documents were worked out and despatched. Then 97 people from six continents, 20 of whom were Chinese, met at Louvain and after a few introductory speeches divided themselves into five working parties. Face to face with the Chinese giant, the differences between the confessions suddenly spread like ants. The mutual question and interpretation was amongst the most significant events of the meeting.

Louvain with its Catholic university is still influenced to a certain extent by the spirit of Cardinal D. Mercier (1851-1926), who endeavoured to "philosophise on behalf of modern man", to bring faith and science into harmony, to dissimilate prejudices at the famous discussions in Mechelen with the Anglican Church, and to remove any obstacles which barred the way to unity. In 1925 he delivered the famous speech about "L'église anglicane unie, pas absorbée", whereby the Anglican Church could have its own hierarchy and keep its own rites, and only

145

be united with Rome at the head. On the occasion of the visit of the Anglican Primate, Dr Coggan, in 1977, Pope Paul VI said that this idea was no longer merely a dream. Even now another Utopia in the same Mercier-spirit could still be built in order that a new approach to the problems, of which China is one of the foremost experiments, be found.

In the introductory speech, Fr J. Kerkhofs, secretary of Pro Mundi Vita, spoke about Mao and other famous men in history. He explained how history can be regarded as the privileged setting for God's revelation. According to a believer's interpretation, God appears, questions and speaks in historical events. For Christians, the entire history of mankind is a holy history as well as history dramatised on stage, where sin and salvation, especially collective sin and collective salvation are acted out.

Consequently, the purpose of the series of discussions was to read and comprehend the "gesta Dei per sineses", what God has taught the larger states through the Chinese nation. However, the teachings of the faith on Creation and Redemption cannot simply follow their course in an abstract void, otherwise they would be both fruitless and absurd. Because of the danger of double meanings they must be considered in the light of what was happening in China. Just as the Jesus phenomenon is interpreted differently by Jews, Christians and Gentiles, so could events in China have a very different meaning for Marxists and Christians. But there is still room for dialogue by remaining open to any other possible interpretations.

Then they set to work. The first working party had as its theme "The new man in China". On the basis of quotations from Maoist texts and of the actual methods of education from nursery to university, it was concluded that the whole education programme was aligned with political values, with the furthering of the nation as a whole and therefore went against all selfish individual interests. Heroes, as well as their shocking counterparts — caricatures of selfish people — were held up as models in books and films. Agricultural and manual work had just as important a place in the curriculum as intellectual work, and therefore people who worked in the administration and in the towns were sent to do agricultural work from time to time. Women were on exactly the same level as men as regards their rights and duties as well as their work. Sex-appeal was taboo, cosmetics were unknown. Thus it can be recognised that other models of good people in addition to the historical Jesus are possible, and that Christianity does not have the monopoly, but acts rather as a critical yard-stick. It was recommended that a halt be called to the distribution of naïve, badly informed news about China, and that it would be better to make an honest criticism of ourselves and to narrow the gulf between christian teaching and christian practice. We must have an increased understanding of the christian life as an "exodus", as a movement of revolutionary optimism and of human devotion to others.

The second working party discussed faith and ideology in the context of new China. Here there was an awareness of the complexity of the theme, and a warning was given against simply comparing faith with Christianity and ideology with China. A fair amount of ideology is to be found in Christianity, just as a fair amount of faith is to be found in China. China, with its community spirit, its distribution of goods in the common interest and its high public and private morals is regarded as a real challenge to Christianity. The fact that this has all succeeded without reference to God and religion raises very serious questions for Christians. The Chinese leadership believes that religion is an anachronism for modern, scientific man, and that it is a relic of feudal idealism. In fact religion has often functioned as an ideology and has interfered with a concern for the state and for the unfair structure of society. However, it is disputed that Christianity is anti-science and reactionary. The Chinese, flexible as they are, are expected to revise marxist-leninist "dogmas" in relation to religion in the course of time. After all, China has never had a strong religious tradition. Confucianism is more a type of humanism and has made it easy for Maoism to carry through a total secularisation. Religion is simply not "needed" any more. Thus religious dialogue with China in the near future is hardly to be expected. However, it is essential that we make extensive revisions to our own religious language in order that it be brought into line with modern thought. Nevertheless, by experiencing his own limitations, a person still remains open to the unlimited, to the transcendental, to the absolute future. Christianity can no longer be presented as religious dogma and a system, but rather as consisting of a group of believers, optimists, radicals and people who are seeking to transform the world. It is only by these means that we can sway and perhaps open up new discussions with China.

The third working party sought to investigate the relationship between revolutionary antagonism and christian love. They reasoned that the removal of any sort of degrading life-style is a part of God's divine plan and that the Chinese experiment can therefore be seen in this light, even if it does not totally and definitively fulfil this divine plan. Christians must take the social aspect of christian love seriously and must identify "out of love" with the poor and not with the privileged classes, who so often exploit the poor. Christian atonement and reconciliation must not happen in the abstract, but should seek to alter the structures. In this way christian love does not exclude the "struggle" against abuse. The dangerous opposite of love is not so much hate as apathy and resignation.

China and salvation history was the theme of the fourth working party. Despite all the deficiencies of Chinese society, it is believed that China is a symbol of God's struggle with the world to carry through his divine plan. It is here that one quarter of humanity has been given a way of life and moral values which, although "unwanted", reveal something about the characteristics of the kingdom of heaven. "We believe that God is present in this process of laborious struggle, and that he is fighting and wrestling to direct their efforts towards a decent goal, and to make his beneficial love a historical reality for all humankind…". Concerning that which has happened over the last 25 years through fear, joy and heroic struggle towards rebuilding the Chinese nation, "we believe that we can see a greater power than China at work, a power which surmounts, yet works within history. This power makes China a sign for the nations, a sign of God's concern about mistakes and abuses which threaten to ruin the foundations of his creation; a sign that in his unchanging love, God is tracing out the path of humankind's history and is leading it towards a new creation". The serious question still faces the churches, which are still so ego-centrically aligned with the western world and its structures, as to why poor nations look so full of hope towards China and not towards the churches. Contact with the people and serving instead of ruling are evangelical principles which are practised more in China than here. We should not be asking ourselves when China's doors will be re-opened to us, but rather when are we going to open the doors of our hearts to China's teaching.

These reflections were taken further by the fifth working party which considered the implications of new China on the understanding of the Church. By this was meant that the Church — in comparison to China — does not include the people, youth and women enough in its "policy making"; that the christian schools in the missions served to a large extent as spring-boards for personal careers; that the churches live in a constant schizophrenic state between their documents and reality, between their teaching of "love thy neighbour" and their tolerance of exploitive systems; that their changes result mostly from the pressure of outside events and are thus seen as God's ruling, rather than from the Church's own prophetic power. Before the churches can hope to offer evangelism to China as something authentic, they must firstly become a lot more radical. When asked, "When can the Church move back into China again?" Fr Herbert Dargan answered with the counter-question: "When will *we* be ready to return to China if necessary?"

Not all readers will agree with these statements. Even in the working parties there was not always unanimity. But they had to be stated one day to modify our biased judgements and not to judge China for once, but rather to judge ourselves in the light of China. In Louvain one had to accept the terrible fact that in China the individual is far too subordinated to the collective, and that this enormous nation has kept itself aloof from all forms of infiltration.[63] Nevertheless, what these 97 Christians and specialists said about China's experiment cannot be taken lightly, that with reservations — as was the case in the Old Testament with "God's ordained" fall of the devil — the greatest of "God's leading nations" in the present day salvation history is represented.

What this fifth working party brought to light in their considerations and interpretations was not voted by the Plenum at the end and not issued in the sense of decisions or even dogmas. It was simply presented to the Churches as a basis for further discussion and study. A sequel — a follow-up — was called for, and it was suggested that the results should be made known through articles and that further meetings should be held to discuss the problem. An "awareness of China" must be created in the christian world.

Professor J. Hsih of the Gregorian University in Rome instigated one of the many sequels. He invited four of his colleagues, professors at the university mentioned above, and two laymen to look into the question of China each from his own specialist point of view.[64] The studies were published in book form. The prevailing tone of the book was one of admiration, sympathy, awareness of a challenge. Julia Ching refrains from associating Maoism with Christianity, from comparing Mao with Moses, from seeing God's Kingdom in new China, and even from maintaining — as does J. Needham — that China is the only real christian country in the world today. "In dialogue it is not necessary to force our own terminology onto the other, but rather to find common ground. Thus, in our case, to find human rather than christian values. A basic example is the maoistic optimism concerning the human person and his potential for development. Through a new interpretation of Genesis, Christianity could promulgate a similar optimism à propos humankind and the Creator".

On the other hand, Paul Rule answered in the affirmative to the question as to whether Maoism is open to infiltration. Whilst in China it seemed to him as if he was living "in the greatest novitiate of the world", yet "I do not see this in the pejorative sense for which the national fantasy blames the religious orders (unhappiness, inhumanity, outward conformity, etc.), but rather in the sense of the deepest human commitment, of the joy in sacrifice, of self-discipline in the light of higher values" (n. 46). Rule believes in a functional analogy between Maoism and religion (the Red Book as a holy scripture, conversion, pilgrimages, Mao-cult, the claims on the deepest essence of a person's being, revolutionary idealism as a faint hope). If China is definitely anti-religious, this accounts for why it does not tolerate its close rivals. "If that is not religion, then it is at least not far from being so" (n. 65). Such a statement has a wider connotation than mere theory. Any missionary approach in the near or distant future will not be initiated from the outside, but rather through the means of maoistic language. In China we will not be preaching to atheists, but to followers of an unmistakably totalitarian religion, which does not make the hope of conversion any easier.

Professor G. O'Collins sought to compare the risen Lord with China, and to ask himself what the christian faith had to say to such a comparison. He found that the suffering of the missionaries then and the suffering of the Chinese nation had a lot in common with Christ's suffering. However, he pointed out that suffering in pre-communist times was a great deal worse and that in the first half of this century 40 million Chinese were killed through wars, bandits, hunger and floods. For the "Christians of the West" all these sacrifices remained an anonymous quantity and it was only as the "evils of Communism" began to rage that people began to react. Most of the numerous heroes who are held up before the Chinese nation laid down their lives for others, which is associated with Christ and with Paul's principle of there being strength in weakness.

Professor D. Grasso was even more optimistic when he wrote, "A Christian can only be pleased with the great economic, political and social progress which has been made in China since 1949". He then clearly indicates that this only amounts to one aspect of what Christ means by salvation. Marxism asserts that death is only a problem for those who still revolve around their own selves. This "self" must, however, be totally involved with the working classes who are the ultimate. Jesus gave a different answer to death. Amongst the many "christian" values in China, the most important value — that of Christ and his trust — is missing. Thus it is impossible to describe China as a "christian" country. The message which China conveys to us is to recognise the greatness of the human person, who, without wanting and admitting to the fact, is the greatest creator. But the human person, great as he is, cannot continually avoid the question of the ultimate meaning of life and history. "We can go yet further in our optimism. It is not only human nature with its questioning which will lead the Chinese to exchange views with Christianity, but we also believe that by creating a just society, Communism has paved the way for Christianity". For the more a person develops, the more he is aware of a "yearning for the totally opposite" (M. Horkheimer). Thus when the time is right, a religious life will re-awaken in China, as is happening in Russia today.

Professor F. A. Sullivan started from the "working hypothesis" that the sensational news about the different

China is true. If in fact it is true, he believes that in view of human nature, which always tends to be selfish, the creation of this society which stipulates fraternity, equality and welfare for the poor represents a deliverance from sin and egotism, which must be seen as the work of saving grace. The expulsion of missionaries did not include the expulsion of the Holy Spirit. Wherever the fruits of the Spirit are to be seen, so also are his works to be expected. To an extent a characteristic of the new person in new China is charity, and this is certainly not this person's self-creation, but is rather a fruit of the collaboration of the person and God's Spirit, which creates and delivers.

Professor R. Faracy, finally, believed that the contemporary individual's deepest aspirations are expressed in Mao's collection of thoughts, that they are a "sign of the times" for us, and that they must also be studied in fundamental theology where Christianity is defended, not only in the light of a possible evangelisation of China, but also with regards to a further development of our own christian society.

The four professors mentioned above are "theorists" in this respect. None of them knows China from within. But what they have said stands as a model attempt as to how teachers of today, each according to his own subject, are trying to understand the Chinese phenomenon and to introduce it into lessons. No realistic theory which interprets God's acts of salvation can ignore the events in China.

We should not suppose that the christian efforts of interpretation at Louvain and Rome would be taken lightly by the Chinese. Similar beliefs are by no means a prerequisite for dialogue. The Jews accept our interpretation of the Old Testament concerning Christ just as unwillingly as the Hindus accept our message that they are saved through Christ. This does not prevent discussion where there is a respect for the opinions of others. For the time being we must leave the Chinese the right to be themselves. We must not include them amongst Christians against their will. This would only produce a psychological shock. Of course, this is what the prophets did. But apart from prophecy, there is also the way of dialogue — tact and understanding of the time tells us that often, and for a long time to come, the second mode of expression should be chosen. In fact it can be foreseen that later christian historians will portray Mao and similar figures in the same way as Old Testament prophets spoke of the pagan king as "the rod of my anger" (Is 10:5), "Yahweh's servant" (Jer 27:6), "Yahweh's saviour" (Is 44:28—45:1).

More directly important than theological discussion with China is the question: What can we learn from China? Before we put forward something christian to China, we must first learn a great deal from this country. This mutual process of learning and teaching will not succeed on a theoretical level, but in actual fact and reality.

There is one city which stands face to face with China, and if nobody else were called to hold a real dialogue with China, the task would befall the city of Hong Kong. To arrive there in November, the most beautiful time of the year, is to experience real paradise; pleasant temperatures, clear spring sun, green sea, blue sky, whole coastlines of sparkling white tower blocks, idyllic bays with magnificent villas and yachts, a dense network of roads over the numerous hills, hotels and shops at the stock exchange, bustling life, noise and children's laughter, for half the 4.5 million inhabitants are under 20.

Seemingly, a shining contrast to outlawed China, a place where life is enjoyed. Yet when you look behind the scenery of this beautiful stage you get underneath this thin film. Almost half a million are very rich, a good half million are middle class, whilst 3.5 million work to stay alive. A few large trusts govern the economy and also pressurise the English administration. Here are the seeds of capitalism in its virtually pure form. Trade unions are very weak, a large proportion of factory workers are moved on annually to prevent them from climbing up into a higher wage bracket and from forming organised resistance groups. Whoever makes the slightest move to rock the boat is liquidated. The problem of poverty and equality of all is by no means solved; neither is the problem of drugs, crime, corruption and prostitution. It is thought that there are 300,000 drug addicts, 28,000 prostitutes and 80,000 members of criminal organisations. Typical symptoms of western affluent society! If one had the freedom to choose, not according to selfish interests, but for the good of the people, there must be serious questioning as to which model would be chosen: China or Hong Kong. The decision would certainly favour China.

Meanwhile things are happening in Hong Kong "as were in the days of Noah". For as in those days before the flood they were eating and drinking, marrying and giving in marriage, until the day when Noah entered the ark, and they did not know until the flood came and swept them away, so will be the coming of the Son of Man" (Matt 24:37-39). As an analogy, it could also be said: so it will be *until* the coming of the Son of Man, i.e., for all time. However, communist China seems to have understood that it is not enough to negligently make a bare living and not to care for others.

The Churches in Hong Kong are a minority: 250,000 Catholics and 200,000 evangelical Christians. Through the schools, hospitals and charity organisations the Catholic Church in particular constitutes an important part of city life as regards buildings and effort. More than a quarter of all school children attend Catholic schools, more than one-fifth of the sick lie in Catholic hospitals. But does the Church also play as important a rôle as the critical conscience of society and as the prophet amongst the children and their parents who pay such high fees? Is at least the Church, as opposed to the city, taking China, their neighbour, seriously?

The general feeling amongst the priests over 40 years of age — foreigners and natives — who went through the drama of the expulsion of the missionaries is this: in China the rich are poorer than the poorest over here. Over

155

there exists no freedom, no religion and nothing to eat. The news about China's progress is a myth which will soon collapse. Only those who are badly informed can think well of China. They are as sure of their knowledge of China as they are of their message about the morals of marriage. "He who says the Chinese are basically the best Christians in the world should be sent to a psychiatrist". In reply to this statement came resounding laughter of approval. When questioned whether the Church in Hong Kong should increase its activity, they reply that the Church should not become involved in politics.

Apart from these self-confident people, for whom China is only a trifle which will soon be dealt with, are the questioners, youth, priests, nuns and students who are of a different opinion. They believe that religion as a rite has disappeared in China, but that it continues to exist as an inward questioning in the human person, and that China has a divine significance for the Church. They admit that in the first place the mass poverty must be overcome not through religion, but through technology and the removal of myths, but that religion will return sooner or later. These circles are trying to form small groups in Hong Kong and to prepare for Day X when the Christians will have to live without priests.[65]

We must accept, as does this younger group, that Communism must destroy a certain form of religion, but that it cannot uproot the last religious seed; that we can promise salvation to the Chinese because they are doing God's will, and because, without knowing they are acting as Christians, they are doing a lot for the poor, ill and homeless; that their secular "experience of God" is a challenge for us Christians and is a new chance for the Church; that we are waiting in hope for the day when we can freely pass on the glorious message amongst the ascetic everyday life of the Chinese nation again, to tell that John the Baptist preached repentance, but that Jesus of Nazareth celebrated the feasts and that the Messiah's time for celebrating has now arrived.

14

Subversive Members of Religious Orders in the Philippines

HONG KONG is not the only place where the western world is being challenged by China. A thousand kilometres away, which is very near for Asia, lie China's neighbour, the Philippines, the only Catholic country in Asia, which obviously has a special rôle to play. The Philippines cannot be simply concerned with themselves since they stand on Asia's threshold. They are being judged as to what extent Christianity is able to benefit the development of a nation and a society. As the Jews set a divine example as a chosen people and as a monotheistic island amongst the pattern of nations in those times, so should and must the Philippines interpret their position in Asia in a similar fashion.[66]

Until about 1970, the Philippines had been fulfilling this rôle well. Earlier, the Filipino Church resembled a caricature rather than a model. Those outside the Church could use all their stored-up arguments against such an institution as was to be found there. Even critics within the Church spoke of the Philippines as a satellite of the Latin-American Church from the good old days. A deep belief and a great reverence for all the madonnas and saints could be seen here, as well as magic, an egocentric conception of religion and a legalistic, clerical and triumphant Church which had successfully protected itself

157

from all attempts of revival for so long. Whoever sought to undermine the established system immediately felt the strong hand of the state or church authorities. The numerical proportion of priests to believers of 1:7000 was on average less than the Latin-American proportions of 1:5000 and this because the Spanish clergy believed in pleasing themselves and did very little to promote a native clergy. All these factors worked towards the creation of a state and apathetic Christianity in the midst of a world in revolutionary change and within a nation of young people (50% of the population are under 17 and 83% under 40!), who were anticipating a new future.[67]

Added to this was the disastrous uniting of the Church with the feudal system. The accusations and reflections of the leader of the Filipino Communist Party, A. Guerrero (his real name is Jose Ma Sison; he lived in the underground and was captured by the police on November 20, 1977) were neither complimentary nor wrong. He pointed out that the 50 richest families had the most part of the land and money at their disposal, and that 0.36% of the population owned almost 50% of arable land. Whoever rented land from them had to give up 50-80% of the harvest.

For four centuries bishops and the old orders, who had also been given large areas of land, were the trustworthy defenders of the system, and they explained the divine basis of the land laws, whilst at the same time they were treated with great care by the landlords. They owned their palaces, throne-rooms and privileges and seemed heedlessly happy with all they had. No wonder A. Guerrero came to the conclusion, "the revolution of the 700 million people in China has made this country into a bastion of socialism. We are glad to live so near to this nerve-centre of the world revolution of the proletariat!"[68]

Thus, unless the overdue revival of such a society and Church was to be left up to the Communists, something had to happen from within the Church. Strength had to be found to set about questioning the status quo

158

and to expose the injustices embodied in the system. They had to put up with being criticised and condemned by the guardians of "authority" as being "subversive". But the fact and the truth of the matter was that they were seeking to establish a God-given system worthy of humankind.

This difficult and by no means isolated process began in about 1970. It was then that the first all-Asian Bishops' conference took place in Manila at the same time as a visit by the Pope. Both events gave the revival of the Church and society a necessary impetus (cf. Chapter 7). The bishops took part in a preparatory session for the 1971 Synod in Rome concerning justice in the world and in the Church and which then went on to make grossly "subversive" statements that action for justice should not simply happen incidentally, but was a "vital element of evangelism itself".[69] By this time already 100,000 members of the "Cursillo de cristiandad" in the Philippines were prepared for a new form of Christianity which was the nucleus of the revival. In the same years many orders and congregations held their annual general meetings to pass on the new impetus to the front lines. Thus there was a gathering together of all the different groups in all levels.

The real starting shot took place at a meeting in Manila in 1971 of the superiors of the male and female institutions in the Philippines.[70] As the spokespersons for the prophetic Church, the assembled priests and nuns first gave an account of how they had an enormous responsibility and that until now they had been living carelessly in a western fashion, their many schools being at the service of the fee-paying middle and upper classes, and without once taking into consideration the uncertainties and problems of the poor who made up 85% of the population. Thus they had been spending their time "isolated" on an island, removed from harsh reality, condemning the timid demands of the people for more justice, and themselves being condemned along with the Church as being part of the oppressive structure. Now they saw the light and questioned whether the time had come when God was "revealing" through the signs of the times what he wanted to say in a situation where the rich and poor in a "christian" society were divided in such an unchristian manner. The sting of such questions went deep, and abruptly awoke many from their previous slumber.

The following year on September 21, 1972, the whole situation was made critical by the declaration of martial law. The previous day 6000 "suspicious" people, mostly prominent politicians, were imprisoned. President Marcos' strong hand certainly brought the earlier political chaos to an end, but at the same time, by curbing the right to democratic freedom and to similar factual information, it was an insult to humankind. He announced great programmes for land reform, which came to a halt after achieving less than half of what had initially been anticipated. He boosted the economy, not in the interest of the poor, but in the interest of those who were already rich, as well as the multi-national companies. He removed people from the barracks and slums in order to erect in their place hotels and magnificent pleasure grounds for prestige and foreign tourists.

The superiors of the orders were no longer satisfied with simply analysing and protesting against this situation. In 1973 they began to form "task forces", groups with a specific task, e.g., one group took on the task of using underhand methods to contact political prisoners and of giving relatives necessary information; another group was ordered to edit the magazine "Signs of the Times" to supplement the open media's biased information, and to formulate due criticism of the government and Church. In 1974 another group carried out a study of workers' conditions on the sugar plantations. The results showed that barely 40% of the workers received the minimum wage as set by the government, and that whereas the average worker could only buy four measures of rice with his wage in 1962, now he could only buy two measures, etc. Another group was urged to take on the task of increasing the awareness of those who lived in the slums and country. The nuns were extremely well adapted to carry this out. Many congregations closed their schools to leave the nuns free to do this work. Four or five nuns now live together in normal houses amongst the poor, not to be charitable towards them, but to make the poor aware that they were not second class citizens and that with a strong will and through their own efforts they could improve their clothes, living conditions and their lives, and that through this they themselves could turn the wheel of development. In this way "basic christian communities" were formed, where religion was integrated into daily life and took on a meaning again. The Sunday services of such communities — with or without priests — were not only a devout experience, but also had a stimulating effect on day-to-day life. The Sisters who were prepared for this work in various seminars are today more open and radical than many priests who are absorbed in their work in structured parishes. On the whole the people reacted very well. It was ascertained that these people's groups could be formed elsewhere, and the Sisters are thinking of leaving the running of the groups up to the people themselves and of carrying out the same process again somewhere else. Even the Sisters who remained in the schools have been infected by the new alignments. They are now seeking to do whatever is necessary to turn out pupils as involved Christians and not simply as egoistical aspirants.

The majority of the superiors of the orders went along with this new course of action, but a minority remained disunited. This situation was the reverse as far as the bishops were concerned. The minority supported the government who viewed this new advance as being "subversive" rather than constructive. This anxious group informed Rome, which resulted in the Congregation for Religious sending a letter via the Nuncio on April 17, 1975 to the male and female presidents of the Union of

Superiors, stating their concern about "the unfortunate turn of events ... the almost exclusively socio-political overtones ... the statement in open opposition to the hierarchy".

At the end of that year, the apostolic exhortation *Evangelii nuntiandi* came out; it took up, developed and disseminated the themes of the Bishops' synod in 1974. The Bishops' synod made very bold statements about the urgency of evangelical testimony for the salvation of the world, about the two dimensions of this salvation, the historical, the worldly and the eschatological, and about the priorities of the laity's tasks in the world of politics, economics, culture and knowledge and that accordingly priests should urge the laity to act and not simply to pray. The members of the religious orders of the Philippines held a meeting about *Evangelii nuntiandi*, and expressed anxiety about the discrepancy between the Church's documents and its practical bearing. The cause of the disunion between them and the hierarchy was seen as being not so much on a political as on a theological level, that is, in the varying interpretations of salvation, which can be interpreted as being either traditionally supernatural or as newly integrated.

On October 25, 1976, the respective Congregations for Bishops and for Religious Orders sent a further letter in which the members of the orders were strongly criticised and the bishops were urged to enforce their authority to re-establish unity in the Church. The letter, which was then manipulated by the government, caused astonishment not only amongst the members of the orders in the Philippines, but also in the Union of Superiors in Rome.

In the meantime, a group of 17 had formed in the bishops' conference which later increased to 25 (out of a total of 62 bishops), who totally agreed with the attitude of the members of the orders, and who themselves made very clear declarations about people's rights and the correctly and wrongly interpreted "unity of the Church" (their document of November 4, 1976). It was also too

162

much for the bishops when, during 1976, four missionaries were expelled without having the opportunity to justify themselves, more and more people employed by the Church were imprisoned without trial and finally two radio stations were closed down and the two magazines, "Signs of the Times" and the "Communicator", were banned. In their January meeting in 1977, they produced a joint document which spoke of the "painful irony" — that in this country with such a great potential there is so much mutual suspicion and that the divine right to preach the whole gospel is not being safeguarded ... . In the end the Church was unified and, in fact, along the new lines!

But behind the scenes the disharmony continued. It could hardly be expected that the whole Church could be as "one" in such a critical situation. If pluralism has already become a fact theologically and has been proven, then it must be proven all the more in socio-political attitudes. According to sociological backgrounds and theological opinions, not all the bishops "can" be of the same opinion here. These frontiers of human existence must be simply accepted. Each has the right to maintain his point of view, but at the same time he should have an understanding of the opinion of others. They should not all exercise prophetic "subversive" action at the same time. Not everyone has the same charisma. It would be wrong to understand and to force the unity of the Church into a narrow gauge of uniformity, whilst at the same time describing everything else as "disunity". True unity is achieved through multiplicity, and the spirit of unity ensures that the various groups remain in discussion and do not degenerate into a polarization.

Cardinal Jaime Sin sought to direct the Church into a sensible middle path. In an interview[71] he admitted that until now the government had not implemented a single project which would benefit the rural population. He was equally of the opinion that eternal salvation cannot be genuinely preached without being seriously engaged in temporal salvation. He was not seeking to move the

Church on from "uncritical involvement" to "critical opposition", but to at least a "critical involvement". Although he could not go continually to the President — without losing his credibility — he had nevertheless already stated many of their grievances, and amongst other things he had said that he was relieved that the missionaries were talking, for without this valve there could well be an explosion.

It is unfortunate that after all these great hopes, in 1977 Fr B. A. Mayo, SJ, the President of the Union of Major Superiors, was ordered to return to the USA for a "sabbatical year" by the Roman authorities, and Sister Christine Tan, President of the Sisters' Union, could not be re-elected. Thus both groups were robbed of their strong leadership. But this deadlock was overcome. Life continued on a practical level. The still small minority with its new way of thinking has a short history, but a long future. The other groups have long histories but short futures. The times are working in favour of the Church, which will no longer be the way it was, but is being led by the documents of Vatican II, by *Populorum progressio* and *Evangelii nuntiandi*, and is being challenged by the signs of the times to follow the new path so that the Filipino nation need no longer look to the Communists for the fulfilment of their hopes.

A small pause is worthy of mention. On September 23, 1977 a peaceful protest march was held by farmers and students demanding again that martial law be brought to an end. A number of members of the orders were amongst the protesters. Suddenly the police arrived, spraying staining water into the crowd. They were aggressive and took many people, including 16 nuns and four priests, away in cars to headquarters. The fact that they had traces of water stain on them sufficed as evidence that they had participated in the "illegal meeting", and that they had to answer before the law for "subversive activities". During the trial held at night, the police at first tried to frighten the nuns with the threat that they would tell their superior everything. Then an undaunted sister answered, "Go ahead and notify her — I am the superior". In the morning the house arrest was dropped after an appeal. They all wrote their defence statements in which extracts like the following can be read: "I, the undersigned, declare that nobody in the march was carrying weapons, that everything took place in a peaceful atmosphere until the police intervened and without any prior warning sprayed the demonstrators with water, whilst others with shields and truncheons hit innocent bystanders. ... The police told us to get into the car. We did not do this voluntarily. They did not dare push us in with force. So we stood there for a long time, saying our beads and singing religious songs. After a certain period of time a bus arrived carrying policewomen, who explained to us that we would not be taken to prison. So we got on. ... I rejected any accusation of subversive activity. The fact is that I only joined the masses to give the poor and suppressed a helping hand, to practise justice, to express my beliefs and be responsible for the weak and helpless of our society. I am also personally convinced that only grievances justified openly can make positive progress with the government ... . I joined the students, workers and occupants of temporary homes in their demand for human rights simply as Christ had done, since a pledge for justice is an essential part of the preaching of the gospel. I observed the exhortation of the first united Asiatic Bishops' Conference here in Manila which recommended that the dialogue with the poor should be practised and not merely preached. I felt that it was my right and my duty to demand human rights, since even the Minister of Justice, Fred Ruiz Castro, at the World Justice Conference stressed that human rights were to be guaranteed in the Philippines ...". A Church which has followers such as these will not only survive but will do much for other Churches.

The action on this basis is prepared by systematic courses on the organisation of the guilds and the method of creating an awareness, etc., for example, in the "Institute for Social Order" of the Jesuits and it is intensified in the "Asian Social Institute", a research institute which is considered as the technical branch of the Church, even if it does exist side by side with it under constant — probably unavoidable and beneficial — pressure. Hand in hand with the social "subversive" function, goes the theological "subversive" function which tries to repeat not abstract theology which is stagnating, but to formulate a dynamic christian interpretation which relates to life, to which Vatican II has given the go-ahead and for which it has set the trend.

The "East Asian Pastoral Institute" is the most notable of the many such training centres in the whole country. Its intention is to instil the students with an awareness of the Asiatic environment and to make them conscious of the fact that Church and theology both have a contribution to make here. When the missionaries were expelled from China in the 50s, one of them, Fr H. Hofinger, was convinced that Asia needed a new kind of catechesis and preaching and with a few helpers in Manila in 1955 he began his "Beneficial Agitating Activities" through the medium of a newspaper, reports and organised congresses, and in 1966, from all this, there emerged the present institute. Since then, 3318 priests, nuns and lay people have passed through these places, to all the Asiatic and Oceanic countries, whether on a regular course of one or more years or in aggiornamento courses lasting two months, which are run not only in Manila, but also in various countries in Asia and Oceania. It is highly significant to give a positive meaning to the christian religion in the face of the competition from other religions and Marxism.

We shall therefore make a visit. It is November 18, 1977. 81 people — 37 nuns and laywomen, 44 priests and laymen between the ages of 26 and 59 — sit in the auditorium. Of these, 56 are Asians from 14 different countries, 14 are from 6 different Oceanic countries and 11 are Europeans who work in Asia. One could hardly imagine a more interesting combination.

In comes Professor A. Pieris, a Jesuit from Sri Lanka, the first Catholic priest to possess a doctorate in buddhist studies from a buddhist university. He teaches in Sri Lanka, at the Gregorian University in Rome and in Manila. Today, he gives a synopsis of his understanding of other religions with reference to the Church and the kingdom of heaven.[72] It is precisely this theme which runs like a thread through our book. In short, Fr Pieris makes the following considerations: if one surveys the last four hundred years of missionary history, one can determine four different ways in which the Catholic Church relates to other religions. In other words, there were four missiological experiments which superseded each other. Behind these there were explicit or implicit theological principles, which could be termed: the Conquest Theory, the Adaptation Theory, the Fulfilment Theory and the Sacramental Theory.

The Conquest Theory lasted for the longest period of time. It characterised the great missionary era from the sixteenth century until this century. Gothic spirituality then had to make way for the triumphant baroque. The post-Constantine merger of God's concepts and those of the emperor had reached its peak. Pope Nicholas V only expressed the spirit of the age when, in 1455, he gave a christian king complete freedom and full power of authority to "invade and subdue the country of the Saracens, heathens and other enemies of Christ". The kingdom of heaven, outside which there is no salvation, had become identified with the visible present Church. Missionary work became synonymous with colonisation and the discovery and acquisition of new territories with the conversion and incorporation of the heathens to the Church. Religious tolerance was motivated by love for those people who were assumed to be damned and who, at any price, had to be rescued from the clutches of Satan. The eagerness to save souls went hand in hand with the readiness to become a martyr.

The Church did not need to wait until Vatican II in

order to realise that this course of action "was not in keeping with the gospel spirit or directly opposed it" (*Dignitatis humanae*, 12). The reaction occurred through what could be called the prophets of the Adaptation Theory, from the Italian Jesuits De Nobili, Ricci, etc., to the newer missionary theologians. There was, of course, no real theology involved, but more a human effort to find a better introduction to those religions, i.e., to put the Conquest Theory into practice.

We have to learn to take another attitude from the incarnation of Christ. The Word did not simply externally become Man, but the Word "became flesh" with all its consequences. Therefore, even in Christianity, it is not simply a question of conformity but full acceptance of non-christian religions and their perfection and fulfilment in Christ. This Fulfilment Theory is clearly taught in Vatican II. The respective comments belong amongst the best missionary analyses of the Church doctrine. The whole thing can now be seen in a rational ecclesial context. The Church is no longer the kingdom of heaven realised, but an embryonic kingdom in the process of development (*Lumen gentium*, 5). It is treading the path towards the kingdom (*Gaudium et spes*, 1). The kingdom of Christ is, therefore, a concept which goes further than the Church. The other religions can, therefore, already be seen in the context of the kingdom. They are already "the mysterious presence of God" (*Ad gentes*, 9), even if they still have to be enlightened and purified. They are already tuned into the Church (*Lumen gentium*, 16).

This interpretation is fascinating. Nevertheless, it leaves certain questions unanswered. What then is the difference between the pre-christian nature of the Old Testament and the other religions? We can no longer accept that there grace was instrumental, and that here only nature is. For, wherever a person approaches God, he does it within the bounds of this grace. The other question, however, is this: What, then, is the rôle of the Church which is still a minority institution and in all probability will remain so? In order to be fulfilled in Christ, is it just a case of other religions dying out and being reborn in Christ, or must not the Church also submit to the initiation of Hinduism, Buddhism, etc., just as Christ was accepted by the Old Testament predecessors?

Again and again, the Vatican Council speaks of fulfilment in Christ at the end of time (*Ad gentes*, 9; *Lumen gentium*, 5). This provides the basis for the development of the Sacramental Theory. The Church is repeatedly called the "universal sacrament of salvation". The sacrament is a powerful symbol which manifests God's salvation and puts it into effect. God's salvation, on the other hand, is synonymous with the kingdom of heaven and with God's work through Christ in the whole universe in all periods of history, especially in the enigmatic longing of man for God. Now, however, every religion has this longing and searching for God within man and in his social rites. Amongst all this, therefore, God's salvation is certainly present.

It now falls upon the Church to become the sign of the kingdom of Christ and to interpret for itself and for non-Christians this general and already effective salvation of God in Christ and to make them aware of it. In many cases, therefore, it may suffice for a Hindu to be made a better Hindu because, by doing so, he is brought nearer to Christ, by whom he is already moved, apart from those cases where the Spirit still requires a "Hindu-Christian" himself to become the symbol of the kingdom, while he joins the visible christian community.

The christian God is, in fact, not a God common to all the religions and for this reason, the Church does not have a monopoly on him. He is the Father of Jesus Christ and the Father of all peoples who are all God's peoples. Through the renewal of Communion, the Eucharist, the sacramental expression for it, we Christians are of the opinion that all peoples, even the Hindus, Buddhists and Muslims, by their liturgies and rites are God's people. If it really wants to be the sign and sacrament for all people to be God's people, the Church must become incarnate in those countries. Charge would, therefore, have to be taken of the texts from their holy scriptures in order to make it clear that they relate to Christ. Unfortunately, the Church authorities do not yet permit such a policy. It is for this reason that the Church still stands aloof and is unable to relate on this matter while the people of God outside the defined Church celebrate God's works of salvation, to which the Lord himself gathers them.

We must not forget that the Church itself, like the whole of humankind, is still on its pilgrimage towards the kingdom of heaven. Words like "conversion" and "evangelising" have their meaning not only for the others but also for the Church itself, just as paganism and superstitions appear throughout the Churches. For example, the many Catholic shrines and sanctuaries with their "do ut des" or commercial spirituality obscure the transcendency of the historical God and the radical challenges of the kingdom. Furthermore, we should not preach about the fear of Satan and hell so much, but proclaim the resurrection of the Lord who overcomes all evil. In this respect, the Church must overcome the fear and obscurity of paganism wherever it may be and become the sacrament of the kingdom of joy and peace. Helpful charity activities, etc., therefore, nowadays, are not meant to be restricted merely to the people of the Church, but are for the benefit of all people of all religions and disregarding secondary motives, in this way, are to be secured for the Church.

This Sacramental Theory is not yet sufficiently recognised, yet it will probably not be the last time we hear about it. The awareness that the world is also the world of God's sacrament is becoming more and more widespread. Nowadays, it creates secular "sacraments" like the UN, the Olympic Games, etc., which man makes more and more into the humanity of the God giving them joy and peace. These events must not go against the Church. But with the increasing secularisation of the world — and the Church — the latter will certainly be more of an active catalyst rather than a fixed rock in the future.

We must adjust ourselves to these times where the world is unmistakably revealed as God's sacrament and therefore the Church and the other religions come to an end. The world itself becomes the Church and the kingdom of heaven will then be realised.

The students followed these statements eagerly. For them it seemed like a theological astronaut flight. Does Rome perform the programming and controlling function as does Cape Kennedy in this operation? Apparently not, because the institute met with more difficulties than recognition from the church authorities. And, after all, old theology cannot be spread easily in the present conditions in Asia. Will the master visionary, Teilhard de Chardin, be proved correct in time as was Galileo?

According to the East Asian Pastoral Institute, one really must still visit Radio Veritas. Built with foreign resources in 1963, in order to serve the whole of South East Asia, including China, it remained restricted to the Manila archdiocese for far too long. After the death of Cardinal Santos (1973), serious negotiations finally took place with the other countries, and today, Radio Veritas broadcasts in seven of the most significant Asiatic languages; it is not a programme produced with a restricted outlook but one which has explicit intentions to strengthen the Asiatic awareness and to prepare Asians for the acceptance of values such as brotherhood, tolerance, justice, commitment and courage. Asia seems to know Europe more than itself. And yet, it is important that the Asians get to know one another and meet up with each other peaceably. The many appreciative listeners — people who write in — and the inquiries about the "Open Door" prove that the correct steps are being taken and that the religious issue is in no way being ignored. Every week, about 700 letters arrive just from Japan and 60 a day from Sri Lanka following certain transmissions. From Vietnam, to which programmes are transmitted every hour, morning and evening, many letters request that they should be nevertheless extended because they bring so much joy. In 1978, a programme specifically for China was also begun and the bringing of the "Word of God" to Siberia is also under consideration.

A lot of good things have been said about the Philippines. But that is only a small part of the work done. News must still be spread of the happy increase in spiritual vocations in the last ten years, the increasing number of Filipino missionaries who go to Asia, Africa and Latin America, the Filipino theologians like A. Lambino, C. G. Arevalo, L. N. Mercado and the many Christian Base Communities which are not led just by nuns but also laymen. News must also be spread of the fact that life in Mindanao, for example, and elsewhere has already drastically changed.[73]

One can still ask the strange question: What would have been the consequences if instead of the Philippines, the island realm of Japan had become Catholic? With their intelligence and initiative, the Japanese would probably have tackled the Asian mainland with their belief in a different way. They would probably have run missions in the western traditions whereas for 400 years the Catholic Philippines neither bothered themselves nor others on this issue. But that is now obviously different. It is up to the Philippines to become a centre for the rebirth of Asia and a symbol of hope for Asia. The christian Filipinos cannot think too highly of themselves. As the only christian country of Asia, they are to represent an alternative both for the non-christian religions and Communism. Not that it should be a question of conqueror and conquered, but rather, the Filipinos should "impress" the others and create a climate in which questions on evangelical issues can be brought to them which they, in turn, can try to answer, all of which should not be easily disregarded.

15

The Discovery of the Old Testament in Yalibu

WE would not gain a complete picture if we were only to talk about the classical high religions — as we did previously — these religions that have their great basic forms, their holy books, their temples, mosques and pagodas, and a marked cultural, political and religious relationship. Against this there are pockets of religious groups scattered about and isolated everywhere; there are groups which live much more modestly, without temples or holy books, without any official founder and which are mostly limited to clan and tribal levels. They are accordingly named "primitive" (even though in everyday life they have a fully developed culture), animists (although they do not simply worship spirits but also a supreme God), and an ancient population. These groups have for centuries or for thousands of years shielded themselves, out of some religious instinct or for political reasons, against the surrounding high religions, and have preserved themselves in their own individuality.

An example of this type of group is probably the Bihl in India, with which Fr Charles de Ploemeur[74] made a missionary "breakthrough", or the Jörai on the high plateau in Vietnam, which, despite all their faults, show so much inclination towards God and humankind that Fr J.

Dournes entitled his book on his missionary methods with them *God Loves Heathens,* a book which at the time caused great surprise.[75] In contrast with the high religions, these groups are willing to listen to evangelisation. From these people a large number was recruited into the Church of Asia.

Here we shall be concerned with one of these peoples; in fact, a very small but also very interesting people. It is the people of Kewa, one of the tribes in the southern highlands of Papua-New Guinea (in other words, not in Asia, but in Oceania). These tribes can be considered as the "youngest nation" in the world. During the second World War, when the Japanese occupied the large island along the coast, there were about a million people inland who had no idea that there was a world war, and about whom nobody knew anything. It was only in the 50s that Australian patrols passed through the highlands and brought this group of people out of prehistoric darkness into the light of the world.[76]

People reckon that these Papuan Negroes with their frizzy hair — and therefore quite different from the Asians — came here from an unknown region perhaps 20,000 years ago, and that since then they have lived in the separated valleys, been at war with each other, developed dozens of different languages, have only lived and survived in their own clan and that in all their primitiveness they believed in a God and a purpose for life. The missionaries have been active along the coast since last century, especially those of the Sacred Heart and the Divine Word. The first Catholics to come to the interior of the southern highlands were the American Capuchins in 1955, a group nowadays active in the diocese of Mendi. Out of the whole of Papua-New Guinea, which became an independent state in 1975, 93% of the population of three million people professed themselves as Christians, when, in fact, only 65% are baptised, of which half are Catholics and the other half Protestants. And so a whole nation of "little ones" of the gospel are on the way to Church.

A small number of these "little ones", the Kewa in the region of Yalibu, celebrated a huge feast on December 15, 1977: it was the ordination of a priest, the first native priest of the diocese. For weeks people had worked to decorate the new church on the inside and the outside, and to prepare the numerous pigs for the feast. The new priest did not only have the bishop's hands laid upon him, but he also had the chief tribesman's insignia hung about his neck. There was no end to the rejoicing. The hero of the day, Simon Apea, who was baptised at the age of 11, the second of nine children, had written a 58-page report in the seminary about the pre-christian concept of God in the region of Yalibu. He could therefore draw upon his own experience; yet, he also questioned many old people. We shall now translate a number of pages from this manuscript. The parallels of the experience of God and the thought in the Old Testament can immediately be seen. As the author would say in the conclusion, the same God who was alive in Ur and Egypt also led the Yalibu people in their long history.

The people of Kewa realised that there was someone in heaven who was commanding them to lead a decent life amidst good and evil. That heaven-dweller, known as Yakili, was the person who had created both the world and the human race and had also watched over it. The people on their part were to remain faithful to Yakili, so that neither disaster nor misfortune would hit them.

The word "Yakili" means "good luck" in the Kewa language. This language is spoken by about 80,000 people in the southern highlands. Yakili, however, does not simply mean good luck; to them it means somebody who looks down from heaven. Those who thought about Yakili in their studies and prayers — known as "Yakiliogists" — went a step further and used the word in yet another sense. Yakili does not just sit up there in heaven and look down, but he does everything and provides for everything. For them the complete meaning is therefore "The Maker, Providence". And so Yakili is that being who does everything for the best and provides for everything. Yakili obtained his name from the first man who lived in the region of Yalibu, and who used to tell the tale of how he and his world were created.

This myth was told down the line from generation to generation in a highly exciting way. In time, the people began to question death, suffering and misfortune. Since they had little knowledge of life after death and supernatural powers, they asked themselves the questions: "Where do death, suffering and misfortune come from? Who watches over the world, people and life?" In order to understand these burning questions various myths, stories and legends about the beginning of the world were told. The following myth shows how the people of Yalibu came to worship Yakili as the Creator of the world and of humankind.

"A very long time ago there were four people in the Yalibu valley. Each one lived his own life without knowing the other. Each one with his few tame pigs and dogs believed he was the only person who was living in this area. Yet Yakili had created all of them and had put them in their different places. One day Yakili wanted to deliver an address, and he invited all four of them along. When Yakili appeared in their midst he was half-human and half-vegetation. He delivered his great address, in which he said, 'Pipnua, yaguranua', which means 'lose your skin and live forever'. He ended his address with the explanation of the form of his appearance. Unfortunately, one of the four men, who lived in the eastern region of the Yalibu valley, did not come at the appointed time. He arrived just as Yakili was about to leave. The latecomer asked Yakili, 'Akalaepa?' which means, 'What did you say?' Yakili turned round and said, 'Komanua, ralanua', which means, 'death, multiply'. He added two more words, 'Epeanua, koeyana' which means, 'good, evil'. At that point Yakili disappeared up to heaven and was never seen again".

The meaning of Yakili's unique and mysterious appearance was thus: the part appearance as human showed that human beings are created by him and that they belong to his kinship. It also showed the authority of God over human beings as his creatures. The individual should be under his control and during his trials and tribulations he should take refuge in Yakili, his Creator. This means prayer, sacrifice and devotion on the part of the individual. On the other hand, the part appearance as vegetation meant Yakili's power over the whole of creation. That was quite obvious. He was the keeper and the life-giver to everything that lived upon the earth.

As a result people began to live in families and to experience good and evil. The story of creation was passed on from mouth to mouth. People pondered over what was meant by Yakili's great deliverance. Those who studied the address came to the conclusion that because the first people took part in the creation, Good and Evil were inherent in them. They interpreted the six words uttered by Yakili in a very pessimistic way. According to them the first two words mean a permanent rebirth within one's own life. That means that when a person becomes old, he would lose his skin just as a snake does, and would continue to live. Each time someone experienced this rebirth, Yakili would visit him and would deliver his great address again. In this transition period the Creator would not be called Yakili, but Father, since he is the source of eternal life.

The following two words simply mean Good and Evil because the man from the East came too late to the address. The Yakiliogists say that this absence had destroyed the intimate relationship between God and creatures. The human person could no longer be free from suffering, illness, misfortune and death. The means by which one can be freed from this ill is to offer prayer and sacrifice to Yakili who has the power to do or not to do everything. The last two words mean death and multiplication, the most fatal experiences that a person has to go through in his life. Now a person must lose his complete present form instead of just his skin. Now he knew that he could not escape death. The only alternative that remained was to lead a good life. The event of death, therefore, became a huge secret. People did not know where they would go to after death and whether they would live afterwards and how. Yakili's precedence of death over the first people did not mean the end of humankind. He did not cease to love the people and to provide for them. He did not only say "Death", but also "Multiply". The human race was to be continued. Whenever anybody had to die and had no desire to return to life, someone had to take his place.

From what we have said, we can understand how the people of Yalibu came to believe in Yakili, who created people and the world. The story was never forgotten for it formed the centre of a person's life. The individual needed God for all the necessities of life. He could do nothing without the power from above, the power of the Creator. The cult of Yakili encompassed the whole way of life. As a religion, it was political, economic and social; in other words, Yakili was present and active in every sphere of life. It was widely believed that Yakili lived together with the people. His presence was felt daily. He provided his people with all their needs: rain, sunshine and food in abundance. Whenever they lacked anything, the people prayed and offered sacrifices. Yakili's presence was experienced again and again.

Yet Yakili was not an ancestral spirit, one of the spirits who had died either a long or short time ago. The striking attraction towards Yakili was that he was not the God of an individual or of a family or of a tribe. He was the God of a Kewa-speaking nation as a whole. It was generally believed that there were no other gods besides Yakili. The Yalibu people never worshipped the sun, the moon or the stars as a supernatural being, nor any other gods. Neither the ancestral spirits nor other spirits were ever equalled with Yakili. Yakili was obviously greater and different from these spirits ... .

Following on from this is a comprehensive description of the ancestral spirits, which we summarise here: beside this God of all Kewa, the individual families or clans still had their personal helpers, who were called "Remo" spirits. These were the ancestral spirits. Again, a myth shows how the people recognised the spirits of the dead and how a "non-stop-relationship" began with them. There was once a man who lived with his wife in Yalibu amidst the animals and birds. They had two children. Then the wife died and the father had to provide for the two children who were still young. It was very hard for him. One day, he stood at his door with a heavy heart. Suddenly, a human-like figure was looking at him out of a cloud. A voice spoke from the cloud, "Do not be afraid. I have come to help you". It was his wife, or rather, his wife's spirit. The wife also told him that there must never be any strife or quarrel between them. And so they led a happy, peaceful life and the children grew up. Everything was going fine. One day, however, the man came back tired from hunting, and his wife had not yet prepared the meal for him. He became impatient and began to beat the children. This was contrary to the agreement he had made with his wife. The wife immediately left him and returned to the spirits, but she promised to remain with him in spirit. Whenever he or the children had any problems, they were to offer sacrifices to her and say, "Mother, help us". And so the worship of ancestral spirits was born.

The ancestors live in the world of Yakili, but they also live in the world of the living. They are very close to the living in everyday joys and cares. Whenever the people were planning a war or a huge swine-killing, agricultural work or a celebration of the ancestors, or political discussions with a neighbouring tribe, they always prayed to the ancestors for their presence and advice. It was accepted that the survival of the family or the tribe could not be furthered without them.

On the basis of these spirits people also sensed something about their own life after death, although they had no clear idea what it was. Nobody doubted the fact of continued existence. Nevertheless, the ancestral spirits could not be seen in real life, at the most they appeared in visions and dreams.

In a personally written chapter, the difficulty resulting from the encounter of this old, firm belief with christian faith can now be expounded. One would initially expect people to experience a far deeper knowledge of the Shepherd, Jesus Christ, for no God has ever been so close to human beings as the christian God of the incarnation. But exactly the opposite is true. Simon Apea writes: If we compare the closeness of the traditional religion with the christian religion, the former has more to say than the latter. The question is raised: is the christian religion personal or impersonal? Is the christian God good, or does he behave as an angry father who punishes his children for their misdeeds? The traditional religion of the Yalibu people incorporated the devotion to Yakili and the worship of the ancestral spirits who, although remaining invisible, were nevertheless very close to the people. It was an essential part of the community and it was necessary for the future generation. It acted as a source of inspiration and it helped and guided the whole life of the people.

It was not only the ancestral spirits but also Yakili himself who was present at all family and tribal affairs. He guaranteed a satisfactory solution. On one occasion there was an important celebration in one of the large villages. The week before it rained day and night. On the eve of the celebration, so Simon Apea writes, I heard all the chiefs of the community crying with a loud voice to Yakili: "Father, oh Father, oh dearest Father, watch over us". From that very moment until the following night the rain ceased. The celebration took place on a brilliantly sunny day. From that moment on I, too, was personally convinced that Yakili was in fact present in our small world. Such experiences often happened in the lives of the people of Yalibu. Whenever an emergency situation was imminent, he was called upon by every individual and each group of people.

180

On one occasion my mother and I went to visit relations in the Pangia district. On our way back, when darkness was already descending, we still had two hours to the end of our journey. Then my mother sat down and whispered to someone. I had gone on ahead, but this stopped me and I waited for her. She cried out loudly, "Yakili, oh Father, Yakili, oh Father, do not let darkness fall over us. Give us your light and watch over the two of us". We continued walking, and when we arrived at our village it was still as light as when my mother had started to pray. From these types of experience everyone knew that Yakili was very close to us.

One may ask the question: How does this Yalibu religion stand in relation to the Old Testament? The similarities of both traditions are obvious: a Creator and Lord of eternity who is close to his people, spirits (angels) who are concerned about the good life in the community, and the belief in life after death. Naturally, some differences spring to mind: the Yalibu religion is not directed towards a future messiah and the principle of the covenant of God is less developed. Yet it seems odd that the Jews did not recognise the messiah at the critical moment, whereas, at present, the Yalibuans are almost unanimously accepting and practising Christianity.

A further question which impresses people is that of the existence of the christian God, for his existence is not experienced in the same way as Yakili. They find it difficult to accept the existence of the christian God.

On the basis of the sermon and the words of the Bible God exists only in theory. He created the world, made the first humans — man and woman — and spoke to them in the garden of Eden.

The same God spoke to Abraham, Moses and the prophets, and revealed himself completely in Jesus Christ. But this all took place at the time of the Israelites, in their land and before their eyes. Does not the same God speak in our time, in our country, before our eyes? Does this God also live in Yalibu? How can we determine something about

181

his existence, how to experience him and how to meet him?

These are questions which are swimming about in the Yalibuans' minds. When they see God's work in nature, they believe that this God exists. But is this same God, since he revealed himself in his Son, not as active as he was in the Old Testament? At that time, the Israelites were led to a deeper understanding of their God Yahweh through the experience in their history and through the teachings of the prophets. Certainly at the same time they conjured up a false picture of the future messiah. Their expectations were founded upon human conceptions, and the closeness of God was destroyed. This development was strengthened when the people of Israel were enslaved and ruled by a foreign nation. And so, as a consequence, they finally rejected the Son of God.

The concept and also the name Yakili are valid not only in Yalibu; on the contrary, its fame is widespread. It is found in many languages, even if with different variations. The fact that Christians now use Yakili in their liturgy and preaching makes people realise that Yahweh and the christian God and the God of the Yalibu people is the one and the same.

However, there is still a lot which can be learnt for Christianity from the Yalibu religion. One therefore has to discover the tradition of faith of this primitive religion with great patience and tenacity. In doing so, one has to be convinced that the God in Yalibu was as present and active there as he was years ago in Ur, Egypt and Israel.

Consequently, the closeness and presence of the christian God is a concept which has to be preached with a strong emphasis on the incarnation and the person of Jesus Christ. God has revealed himself indirectly only in the creation and in the Yakili religion, but directly and wholly in Jesus Christ. This means that God wanted to have a relationship with his creatures in a much deeper and more meaningful way. He therefore shelved his godliness and became man. And so God in Jesus Christ is far closer

to human beings than the spirits of the dead. In this way
God can be seen and experienced in Jesus Christ, just as
persons can experience and comfort each other in certain
situations.

For this reason the incarnation does not simply mean
a deliverance from sin, but a being able to bring God closer
to the people and the people closer to God, to foster an
intimate relationship and friendship between God and the
human person. God is not a fierce, rough God, but a forgiving, loving Father, a God who is fundamentally interested in the individual, and is always ready to forgive him
as soon and as often as he is aware of his guilt, and wishes
to return to him. God understands and accepts that the
human person is a sinner. He accepts him as a human being
who lives and acts in a sinful world. This is why God is a
loving, compassionate, forgiving father who welcomes every
sinner. God is not a demanding and an authoritarian father,
who does not recognise the freedom of the individual. He
wants the individual to be able to choose freely, and to do
good out of his own free will.

One should, therefore, not preach so much about God
who punishes sinners in hell, but about God's readiness to
forgive every sinner who is backsliding. Instead of preaching about heaven and hell as destinations for the good and
the bad, one should emphasise in every possible way God's
interest and care for everyone. In this way people will
gradually understand God's love and compassion and will
build these qualities into their own lives. One should also
consider the fact that people will become friendly and
peaceful wherever love, compassion and sympathy reign.
And so, the good God will also make the people good.

So much for Simon Apea's report. One forms the
impression that he remembers very vividly from his youth
the "pre-conciliar" forms of preaching, where nearly every
sermon finished with the promise of heaven but also with
the threat of hell. Moreover, he throws open grave questions
which at the end are only partly answered. How can we
reconcile the experience of the speaking, present God in

the Old Testament and Yalibu's history with the experience of the silent, absent God, under whom modern man is suffering? How can we remove the mythical elements from the numerous myths and yet still retain the fundamental core? How can we enlighten and secularise the numerous human conceptions of God, which were helpful to those people with uncritical minds and a feeling of their own helplessness, without at the same time dissipating everything into a pale image of God, towards which no heart can show any warmth? How can we, against all the autonomy of science, technology, medicine and agriculture, which only provide us with better health and harvests, still experience the all-powerful God; such a God no longer performs the "miracles" of his goodness outside and independently, but precisely *in* these temporal truths and *in* man?

If we ourselves are faced with such a multitude of questions, how much more will those same questions rebound and demand a categoric answer to a people in the midst of its short term transition from a 20,000 year prehistoric era into modern times. Simon Apea has an immensely challenging task before him. Using a beautiful liturgy, he will try to impart to the Yalibu people more knowledge of the speaking, inspiring, close God than was previously possible. He will point out that the worldly truths are the testing ground of the Christian, and he will form a christian community over and above individual clans, in which everyone can feel goodwill and can experience a common effort to the building of a better future. He himself will walk around "like Jesus" and by his presence he will ensure that a new faith, hope and love will materialise. Such a christian religion will then bring back the mythological knowledge of God in the Old Testament and in the history of Yalibu to the essential truth, and will guide it to the knowledge of God in the New Testament and in the future kingdom.

16

The Eastern Religions in the West

EASTERN religions are encountered not only in the East but also in the West and this is something which concerns not only the East, it has to do with the West as well. This encounter is nowadays no longer restricted to the official dialogue between theologians and other specialists but is portrayed in a dozen forms in our everyday life. In all the big cities of the West there are Zen and Yoga centres; we are offered lectures by gurus such as Maharaj Ji, Maharishi Mahesh Yogi and others; we see in public squares groups of Hare Krishna singing and dancing; in the bookshops we find special stands with literature on these religions; and in the supermarkets, post-offices and perhaps even places of work we bump into non-christian students or foreign workers. In an earlier age, Catholic and protestant villages were as cut-off from one another as if an ocean lay between them but nowadays Christians and non-Christians all live in the same society, and it cannot be denied that those whom we used to call "pagans" on average give us a good example of faithfulness to their religion.

Here one can distinguish between the social and the religious planes, each of which has its peculiar problems. The foreign workers present in the first instance a social problem. At the present time there are in Europe around five million immigrant muslim workers, students and engineers. We need them for our economy but we do not accept them as our fellow human beings. They run the risk of losing their human dignity and their religious identity. They are made to feel cold and unwelcome in our secularised atmosphere. There has already been talk of a new kind of slave — in the service of the christian community! The christian skilled-workers in muslim countries are at the head of society, the muslim workers in our countries are in the lowest place. These are facts which give us something to think about.

From November 19 to 21, 1976, there was held in Vienna a pastoral meeting about the Muslims in Europe. A similar meeting took place in Salzburg from February 6 to 11, 1978, and a symposium of a more scientifically theological kind on Islam and Christianity was held in St Gabriel, Vienna, from May 31 to June 5, 1977.[77] In a number of countries there are special agencies which have the function of reducing the harshness of these problems. In Germany, for instance, we have the Ecumenical Contact Office for non-Christians in the archdiocese of Cologne and the Permanent Working Party for christian-islamic relations and for contacts with other world religions.[78] The aims of these efforts are to provide the foreign workers with language instruction so that they can survive better in society; to arrange decent accommodation for them and schooling for their children; to make provision for the recognition of Islam, in addition to the christian Churches and the jewish religious community, as a religion of public law, a step which was taken in Belgium in 1974. Such recognition would permit the muslim foreign workers to levy taxes of their own, to set up social welfare organisations and to perform official public acts such as weddings. Above all it is necessary to create even among our own people human and religious understanding for these men and women. If, for example, Turkish workers were to feel at home in our countries and were to enjoy full religious freedom, this might help to obtain for Christians in Turkey a more equal status.

On the religious level the Muslims in Germany have their most important mosques and centres in Berlin, Aix-la-Chapelle, Munich and Hamburg. In Rome negotiations are complete for the building of a huge mosque one of whose minarets will be, it is said, higher than the dome of St Peter's. After all, we have constantly done similar things in predominantly muslim areas. In the United States there are about 600,000 Muslims (of whom about 120,000 are in New York alone) and plans have been drawn up for a large cultural centre costing 16 million dollars.

In the United States there are also half a million Buddhists. Germany has 8000, England 5000. "Conversions" to these religions do take place. They number thousands but seen in perspective they are no more than a marginal phenomenon. Much larger is the number of those who are favourably disposed towards these religions and of those who are convinced that they can learn something from oriental ways. In Germany it is reckoned that there are 100,000 people practising yoga, 50,000 devotees of Transcendental Meditation and 20,000 of Zen. Undoubtedly, we are only at the beginning of East-West encounter. The age of separation is being succeeded by the age of contacts and of mutual discovery.

Certain circles are reacting to this in a panicked way and are saying that a major onslaught of Islam is in the air, a danger that would be at least as great as that of atheism and materialism.[79] We will hardly get any further with an inverted crusade mentality of this kind. The healing must begin elsewhere. For many Westerners the eastern religions fall into a religious vacuum. By this we mean that "Christians" who have never read the gospels or the writings of christian mystics, who feel a strong antipathy towards church structures and their representatives, who to all intents and purposes have relegated religion to their subconscious and who, finally, are disgusted by the stresses and standards of behaviour of the West, such people make use of, by way of alternative, the

187

non-christian centres in the West, go and spend months in the East, devour books like W. Eidlitz's "Die Indische Gottesliebe", discovering for the first time in such books something of what one might call the experience of God and in this eastern atmosphere of intimacy their eyes are opened.

The best thing to do would be to intercept this movement, to exploit it and to put it into the framework of Christianity. Wise teachers of religion nowadays give the pupils in the upper classes information about these religions and they do this, not only because it forms part of general education at the present time and arouses great interest among the pupils, but also with a view to making dialogue with those of other religions possible and defining more clearly their own position.[80]

Until now this movement has been taking place mainly outside the Churches. This ought not to be the case. In the last twenty years we have discovered one another in the East, are captivated by one another and we exchange our spiritual gifts with each other: why should not this sort of thing happen, in a lesser degree, in the West too? The protestant writer, M. Mildenberger, is able to write: "Many attempts have been made, especially within the Roman Catholic Church, by the disciples of Lasalle and other Catholic theologians who encountered Zen in Japan, to utilise Zen practises for the benefit of christian meditation. In many monasteries — St Augustine's near Bonn, Maria Laach, Beuron, Neresheim, Königsmünster, Niederaltaich are only examples — meditation courses are offered on Zen lines and these are very popular. It seems as if here there is taking place, at least in a small way, a kind of 'blood transfusion' and that the christian inheritance is acquiring new life. At the same time these attempts are the only point at which the religious influences from Asia are being taken up into institutional Christianity even though they still meet with considerable suspicion on theological and hierarchical grounds".[81]

Moreover, a good number of convents of sisters have

not only renewed themselves spiritually through Zen meditation, they have also discovered, as a result of following appropriate courses, a new and meaningful rôle for themselves. Previously they lived a secluded life of devotion, now they have become a focal point and are rendering the Church a real service and can even hope in this way to get new vocations.

The ancient church fathers, especially those belonging to the school of Alexandria, quite naturally made use of Greek — that is to say, pagan — philosophy. Thomas Aquinas had to defend, in the face of opposition, the usefulness of aristotelian-arabic philosophy. Nowadays, the non-christian religions go on their way in the pluralistic world with or without permission. They are standing in our streets and at our doors. Anyone who enters into relations with them or adopts their techniques of meditation, encounters human beings and has an experience similar to that of Abraham with his three visitors (Gen 18) or of the disciples on the way to Emmaus with their travelling companion (Lk 24). For the Lord conceals himself under a thousand forms and reveals himself to the person who shows hospitality to a fellow person and conducts spiritual conversations with him.

17

Balance and Prospects for the Future

AND so the long journey of the reporter has ended. Pen and camera have captured many interesting towns, scenes and insights. At Vatican II the idea was put forward quite "accidentally" that a word might be said about the non-christian religions also. This triggered off a chain reaction of documents, meetings and insights and brought the Christians who represent one-third of the world's population into a fellowship of reflection and prayer with non-Christians, who represent the other two-thirds, in a way which no one could have foreseen. In this turbulent period after the Council, a period which has caused so much confusion and about which so many bad things have been said, one may not, if one is to be honest, overlook the good which has come out of these birth-pangs of a new era.

Before we attempt to formulate conclusions, to evaluate and to get a grip on the individual impressions gained on this journey, we must make certain restrictions. We should not think that we have exhausted our theme. All we have been able to do is give a few dainty morsels. We have not tracked down everything which happens in the field of the religions — to do so one would have to possess the ability to be everywhere — and we have been able to serve up only a watered-down version of what we have seen. We stand there like people looking at the

huge Himalaya range from a distance. We stand in amaze-
ment, impressed, but our experience is very different from
that of those groups who set out to conquer the sublime
peaks. It is said quite rightly that talking about dialogue
is not equal to dialogue itself, and that for true dialogue
knowledge based on experience is necessary and that
dialogue in the full sense of the word is possible on the
two pinnacles of mysticism, between the yogi and the
saint (Dr J. A. Cuttaz).[82] This experience of height and
depth knows no adequate substitute.

To add to our humiliation we have to accuse ourselves
of virtually inexcusable generalisations. All the time we
have spoken only of "the religions" and we slipped in as
it were, Islam, Hinduism, Buddhism. Now these religions
simply cannot be treated in the same way. True, they
all come under the heading "religion", but they are as
different from each other as are roses and lilies or fir-trees
and oaks. K. Klostermaier, a specialist in these matters,
vents his scorn on this kind of theologising when he
writes: "A theology of the modern natural sciences written
by a theologian who has no notion of physics or chemistry
makes a ridiculous impression. Equally ridiculous is a
theology of religions written by a theologian who has no
concrete knowledge of the non-christian religions. The
study of the non-christian religions is at least as difficult
and wide-ranging as that of the natural sciences; and
theologians should not treat this matter too lightly".[83]
Nevertheless, in self-defence we can say that, at the conferences we have described, there were usually lectures
given by specialists which dealt in a concrete way with
the dialogue with Islam, Buddhism and Hinduism and that,
therefore, the abstractions we made did have a solid
foundation. But we ourselves were not able to go into
the specific characteristics; to do this one would need to
have at hand an encyclopaedia and an encyclopaedic
knowledge.

As well as all this, one must take into account that
every religion has its history, in the course of which it has

adopted many new, alien and often even contradictory elements. Especially in the last few decades these religions have, consciously or unconsciously, assimilated basic christian values such as the dignity of the human person, work for the poor, the missionary impulse, the fatherhood of God. The result of this is that in a concrete case one would have to ask whether, for example, one is conducting a dialogue with Hinduism or with the Christianity in Hinduism.[84] We have not been able to make such analyses. We have, therefore, not entered the temples of the different religions with a view to conducting individual studies in matters to do with religion and with the history of civilisation. All we have done is to describe how people of the different religions met one another, opened themselves out to one another and prayed together in temple forecourts, in hotels and in conference centres. All we have been able to do, then, is to give some small idea of something very big, something which is happening before our eyes and which many people have probably not noticed sufficiently.

We would now like to pass on to you a report of the main features of three congresses and other important events at which we were not present. Everyone has heard of Bangalore, and it was there that the "Asiatic Seminar on Religion and Development" took place from July 16 to August 4, 1973. The 84 participants from eight south-east Asian countries were, of course, all Christians and the seminar was directed by Catholic and protestant theologians and sociologists. The "Declaration of Bangalore" approved on this occasion speaks a clear, realistic, almost astonishing language. For instance, in paragraph 8 we read: "In the measure in which we press on with our critical analysis of society and are thrown up against the necessity of bringing latent conflicts to the fore, we discovered the usefulness of marxist methods for the analysis of social reality. From our own experience we know that there is a tendency to force up against the wall and brand as Communists those Christians who with

192

formation of consciousness and organisation aim at radical change, even when they do not accept an atheistic ideology. In the light of the gospel, which is the message of liberation and the source of our faith, we not only oppose this tendency but declare that we, as a christian body, should adopt a more positive attitude to our marxist brothers on social, political and ideological levels".[85]

Chiang Mai is not so well-known as Bangalore, but it is important in the history of Thailand. It was here that from April 18 to 27, 1977, 85 Christians from 36 countries met for a theological reflection on dialogue in community. The aim was to work out how far the christian Church as a community should and could enter into the world community without destroying itself. At the end of this meeting Mgr P. Rossano of the Secretariat for non-Christians in Rome made a statement which is also a kind of balance sheet. He explained that Chiang Mai was a milestone on the road of ecumenism. In future, he said, one would speak of "before and after Chiang Mai". This would happen not only within the WCC but also between the WCC and the Catholic Church. The coming-together of all these Churches is finding its strongest impulse in dialogue with people of other faiths. This, he went on, is a reason for joy because previously the division between Christians has been a frightful scandal for the witness of the gospel. Even ten years ago, the topic of the non-christian religions was an additional seed of division but now agreement has been reached on this matter. From now on all Churches will recognise dialogue as part of the service they render. Dialogue, he explained, can further joy, liberation, certainty, dignity, peace, equality, community and hope. One has to ask oneself now how the agreement on this point can lead on to full communion, and he concluded: "All I can say is that both Churches ought to go forward in their pilgrimage towards the Lord and as a brother I cry out: let us hold our hands out towards each other and let us go forward in the spirit of Jesus. We will find the unity between us and we will further God's family, and all peoples will walk in his light".[86]

It would be worthwhile studying the many visits to the Pope which have been made by monks and official religious bodies from Asia. These visits have been increasing in number over some years and this is due in no small measure to the many preparatory visits made by Cardinal S. Pignedoli all over the world. Anyone who has been present at one of these visits to the Holy Father can confirm that they are real "meetings" of great human and religious warmth. The Holy Father seems at ease among people of such deep faith and he no longer has any inhibitions about opening such meetings with an important prayer. Now one would have to ask and to investigate to what extent these visits are simply a matter of friendly exchanges or whether they contain some hidden, theological pearls which might be taken out and worked over. Just one example. On June 27, 1964, Paul VI received a group of Japanese Buddhists who stated that they were making a series of visits to representatives of the various religions to promote mutual understanding between all "who believe in the supernatural" so that these may contribute to the well-being of the one human race. In his reply to their address, the Pope said, "Your buddhist goodwill-mission is inspired by the longing to further the good relationships between the religions and by your hope of peace and prosperity for all peoples of the different races. We are fully in accord with these intentions of yours. Our prayer, like that of our beloved predecessor, Pope John, at the moment of his death, is the prayer of Jesus at the Last Supper: That all men may be one in complete unity, so that the world may know that you, Father, love them all".[87] If nothing else, it is worth noting that the Pope for the first time officially extends the application of this passage from St John, which was otherwise taken to refer only to unity among Christians, and relates it to all those who are loved by one and the same God and Father.

There are, then, lots of gaps which could be filled, but the most important points have been grasped in this reporter's journey.[88] There is enough, at any rate, to show the new direction and to give now an overall picture of what the various meetings have step-by-step discovered and stated about the non-christian religions, things which are confirmed by the average theology of the present time.

The first conclusion is that we have to bury past ways of thinking and speaking, bewailing, not the fact that they are past but that they were able so stubbornly to assert themselves for centuries. Certainly one should not now go to the other extreme and canonise these religions. There is no such thing as a perfect religion, a religion of pure culture. In every religion (including Christianity!) alongside faith, there is superstition, alongside the spirit: money, alongside mysticism: routine, alongside God: the devil, alongside grace: sin, alongside truth: error. But these global judgements about that paganism and that idolatry (cf. Chapter 2) date from a time when our eyes were blinded by priggishness. For this, we have today to say in their temples an honest "mea culpa" and in our churches a prayer of thanks that in the meantime we have received sight.

In those religions, in their sacred books, in their religious practice, among their monks and mystics there are in fact thoughts, sayings, attitudes to life which simply surprise us, there are pearls which we wonder at, men whom we admire greatly when we meet them. How beneficial it is to discover such men, to speak with them, to pray with them, to know that you are at one with them! They form the better part of the human race; they do not attract attention but they compensate for all the conflicts and crimes and in the storm of the world they, in a prayerful way, give the right answer to the real questions of all human beings. This function for humanity no longer falls only to us Christians as we used to think; it is the common property of all religions.

Now the radiance which shines forth in these religions is the rays of the one Light, Christ. If "all things were created ... for him" (Col 1:16-RSV) and if he "enlightens every man who comes into this world" (Jn 1:9) then Christ must always have been present and effective in the whole of humanity well before the missionaries arrived anywhere and proclaimed him and even in those areas and in those hearts which the gospel has not yet reached or which it has not yet convinced and led to faith. The Father of Jesus Christ was never one to discriminate, he was never a "respecter of persons" as the scriptures tell us repeatedly, almost obstinately (cf. Col 3:25; Eph 6:9; Rom 2:11). The Father has not given bread and grace to the Christians and only serpents and scorpions to the "pagans". Wherever and whenever human beings following their conscience did good, not just by their prayers and sacrifices, but also by their dedicated service to their fellows, their zeal for justice, their bravery in living and dying, they did this already in the order of grace and it worked towards their salvation. To this extent we may take literally and very seriously what St Paul wrote to Titus (2:11): "In this the grace of God has been revealed to us that God wills the salvation of all men". (RSV has: "For the grace of God has appeared for the salvation of all men ..."). That is, in a single sentence, the heart of the christian message which we have to proclaim. That is the good news for everyone. This question of the real possibility of individuals even outside the visible Church being saved was officially settled by Vatican II (*Nostra aetate*, 2; *Lumen gentium*, 16).

To say this includes the admission that God sent the persons belonging to those other religions rays of light, insights; he gave them seers and prophets and let them have a kind of revelation however one may interpret this. As early as the thirteenth century, we find Thomas Aquinas speaking of the "possible providential anticipation of revelation outside the jewish-christian tradition".[89] Now the sacred books of the non-christian religions came into being as a result of that "revelation". And even though they do not carry the seal of authenticity as the word of God like the writings of the Old and New Testament canon, it is nonetheless fitting that we read them with reverence and with a certain readiness in some way to hear from them the voice of God. There are theologians who accept these books as inspired, but this is disputed and fundamentally not all that important a question.[90] However we can nowadays defend our christian claim to revelation and inspiration more honestly if we understand this in a not too exclusive way but recognise a similar action by God in other religions too. Of course the differences would have to be clearly marked out. Taking all the circumstances into consideration one can argue that a theological case could be made for using the best texts from those books in the christian liturgy (cf. Chapter 9). But from a pastoral point of view this question is premature and in the meantime it is forbidden by Church authority.

Connected with the possibility that individual non-Christians can be saved is the further question as to whether they are saved *in spite of* their religion, *in* their religion or *through* their religion. The first view presumed that those religions were only the work of creatures or even of the devil and made no contribution to salvation whatsoever (K. Barth), and that human beings, contrary to all expectations, achieve salvation only through God's free choice, through a miracle of his grace. This view is held by scarcely anyone nowadays and can be forgotten. The second view represents a kind of compromise. It is granted that those persons are right to carry out the rituals and customs of their religion because conscience obliges them to do what the whole community does. But according to this view they are saved not through these rituals but through their own inner religious attitude. This, of course, runs contrary to every reasonable anthropology because a person's life is not only that of an individual but of a being constituted in society. Such a view would react on the christian understanding of the sacraments in that one would have to say that a person is saved not through the sacraments but only by his inner faith, which is both true and false. So then, a theological case can be made for the third view, according to which those religions are channels of grace, ways to salvation and God's one plan of salvation is divided into two successive, or rather, parallel phases called the general and the particular history of salvation. The first of these phases began at the same time as the human race and continues wherever Christianity has not yet reached with sufficient historical impact. The second phase began with Abraham and reached its climax in Christ and in the age of the Church.[91] The saving action of God with "his people" does not exclude, it includes his saving action with all peoples and religions and is a sign and guarantee of this. The two areas are not opposed to each other nor are they identical with each other; they are ordered one to the other and always with Christ as the centre and the climax of all salvation history.

At this point we have to stress once again something that has already become clear, viz that all statements made about revelation, inspiration and ways of salvation are always to be understood in the appropriate analogical sense when applied to the non-christian religions. We do not wish to, nor can we, play-down the Christ-event. This remains a special case, an unsurpassable case, the cause of all similar cases. It is one thing to receive the word which God had addressed to humankind through certain seers, another to hear the decisive word which God has addressed to humankind in Jesus Christ as the fullness of revelation. When we spoke of "salvation *through* the religions", this is to be understood (something which Christians always take for granted) as salvation in and through Christ. No one saves himself, he is saved. Therefore, we still confess that no other name under heaven is given to us whereby we can be saved (cf. Acts 4:12). We cannot give up this claim without giving up our Christianity. Of course, we must remain aware of the fact that this belief nowadays is very much attacked and that we have to be careful how we handle this treasure of belief in the presence of people of other faiths. For Jesus stands with his life and work alongside other similar great people as a fact of world history. His absolute importance cannot be put forward as a thesis capable of being proved scientifically, but is something which can happen and indeed does happen again and again whenever a person in faith and discipleship makes room for this absolute importance, so that Jesus becomes for that person the unconditional and absolute support, influence, determining and fulfilling being. This does not mean that this absolute importance of Jesus is a projection, a product of faith and does not stand on its own. It means that in our world, for us men and women, it becomes an event only when it enlightens a person in faith. Thus I can confess my faith in the presence of people of another faith but not take for granted that they will accept my faith.[92] This leads us to the question of dialogue.

For nearly five centuries we appeared on the Asian scene with our missionary claims and achieved little. But then we learned, above all through the character of John XXIII and the spirituality of Vatican II, that in addition to the missionary, pastoral and ecumenical function the new attitude of dialogue also has its function. This is in no sense simply a change of tactics aimed at getting into the house, so to speak, through the back door. It corresponds, rather, to a new insight, viz that we accept and take seriously the other person as an image of God in his dignity and freedom, his inalienable uniqueness and hence in his otherness and that the meeting of two partners of different kinds serves to enrich both of them. In the past what happened in missionary activity was that individuals were detached from their religious and social unit, had to abjure and lay aside as "reprehensible things" all the values of the religion they had previously practised and adapt themselves perfectly to our society. The same thing happened with the converts from the protestant

Churches. They were enriched by us, but we were not enriched by them. We believed that we already had everything. Today we seek to meet one another in dialogue as groups to discover and to admire one another, to learn from one another and even in a brotherly spirit to criticise one another. We each form one for the other a "constructive opposition" which can only be of good use in overcoming the ever-lurking danger of occupational blindness. We also believe that we can in fact enlarge and enrich one another, since even the Church is only on its way to its eschatological fullness. Dialogue is, then, a value in itself and has its own specific purpose.

In spite of this, dialogue cannot abolish mission. Both functions are to be regarded as complementary not as alternatives. Because of the whole way the Church has of thinking of itself it can never fundamentally give up its missionary claims precisely because in dialogue each party has the right to remain itself. Each of the two functions has its own sound justification but the relationship between them — harmony or unavoidable, healthy tension? — is not yet at all clarified. In Beirut and Nagpur unmistakable efforts were made to find a solution, but the word of enlightenment was not spoken. Pope Paul VI sensed this lack and in his opening address to the 1974 Synod of Bishops, whose theme was the evangelisation of the world today, he mentioned as one of the problems to be solved the tension and unity between freedom of religion and conversion, between dialogue and mission. The Synod did not discuss this problem further and the Roman Curia does not give a good example inasmuch as it has separate bodies for the two functions, viz, the Congregation for the Evangelisation of Peoples which presses only for mission and conversion, and the two Secretariats — for the unity of Christians, and for non-Christians — which speak only of dialogue. Which should one pay heed to? The right synthesis is not yet available neither in the way the Curia works nor in theological reflection. We are still waiting for an exhaustive work on this topic.

Muslims nowadays are demanding more and more frequently — the most recent occasion was the Islamic World Congress in Cairo at the beginning of 1978 — that Christians officially give up their missionary work in islamic regions. To this demand one can give a number of answers. First, the Muslims are assuming that force or cunning is used to baptise individual Muslims and that proselytising goes on. This kind of missionary activity no longer takes place and they are, therefore, tilting at windmills. Secondly, most other religions, headed by Islam, put forward a sort of claim of exclusiveness and, from the other direction, even in the most recent times we hear of crude abuses and proselytising. One example concerns Central Africa where President Bokassa for a while officially declared his allegiance to Islam after President Gaddafi had visited him and brought him a gift of dollars. Thirdly, mission is not only preaching the word, it is above all service for a better world. If you ask Muslims if they would like the sisters to withdraw from the hospitals, they will not hear of it. Fourthly, there are circumstances in which, if the signs of the times, through which God's intentions are made clear (*Gaudium et spes*, 11), indicate it, the Church can in fact forego express missionary work and its aims to convert people. In such a case the Church would content itself with dialogue and not thereby be disloyal to its Master nor would it question the inalienable right to freedom of religion, a right which also includes the possibility of changing one's religion in the light of better insights. But the Church need not exercise all four functions at every time and place and through all its members.

More than 750 years ago Francis of Assisi gave a spirit-filled answer to this question. Writing to his brethren who "under divine inspiration wish to go among the Saracens and other unbelievers", he says that there are two ways of being present among them. The first consists in living simply among them, not arguing and quarrelling, doing good to them and giving them the example of christian living; the second consists in preaching God's word openly so that they allow themselves to be baptised and become Christians. Regarding the crucial point of when one should change from one way to the other, he says, in a classical phrase: " ... when they see that it is pleasing to God".[93] Thus he boldly assumes it can be part of God's intention that, for a longer or a shorter period, one should not preach or engage in missionary work but only in dialogue, preaching the gospel openly when one judges that the "kairos" has come, when one recognises God's will from the sign of the times.

In conclusion, then, we can say that God has always been in dialogue with all peoples and still is. On the basis of the creation he has spoken his definitive "Yes" to the whole human race, a "Yes" which he did not retract but rather confirmed by his "Yes" to Abraham and to Christ. We cannot regard Sinai and Tabor as the only mountains in the world where revelation has taken place. Therefore, in conversation with persons from other religions, we have first of all to listen carefully to see if we can pick up what God has said to them and what he is saying to us through them; and then we have carefully to make known our own contribution. From the very beginning, creation was directed towards Christ and nothing ever came to be which had not this reference to the Word. The existence of Christ has made clear to us this mystery and this connection. For this reason we should not suppress it but should try to make it clear to others as well.

In discussions between various religions one angle came more and more to the fore, viz, that religion is to do with human development, with peace and justice in the world and that all religions together must mobilise their moral forces in order to motivate people to the effort necessary for this. This requires a reorientation of the religions which used to be so preoccupied with the next world that they scorned this one. Already in Christianity liberation-theology has met and is meeting with hostility in certain circles. How much more can we reckon with this in the Asiatic religions! These are faced with the tragic alternative of disappearing if they do not modernise themselves or of losing their soul if they do. Their one-sidedly mystical character and their orientation to an interiority which turns the gaze away from the concrete, the objective and from other people allow no possibility for the individual to be saved also in the midst of social, political and technical realities.[94] These religions have to undergo a radical "conversion to the world"[95] and present the intelligentsia and the youth of Asia with a credible case showing that religion is not opium and alienation but an impulse which makes a life more committed. Westerners, having had too much of and being frustrated by technocratic civilisation, flee to the East and expect salvation from its spirituality. Meanwhile, easterners turn away from the ashrams and regard them as an obstacle to liberating progress. "One can understand these young people who, in the face of the almost apocalyptic dimensions of the economic, social and political problems of Asia, shake their heads at the West which, living in a state of technological and material surplus, nevertheless believes that it has to draw its salvation from the East. One can understand why these young people of Asia open themselves to the ideas of Marxism and why they bid farewell to the religious backwardness which only perpetuates the hopeless social situation and keeps power and wealth for a narrow upper crust at the cost of the impoverished masses".[96] The static religions of Asia, which accept the existing order as the Karma, that is, God's providential disposition, have something to learn from Christianity's new mysticism of creation and its dynamism and this for the good of their peoples and for their own good. If God is father of all humankind, then he is also father of the whole human person and wills the total salvation of his people and not just the salvation of their souls.

We have now covered a great distance, seen new panoramas constantly before us, walked through new valleys and climbed new mountain ridges. The christian minorities, going ahead as an advance guard, have drawn vast hordes after them, so that they were walking along the same road and got into discussion not only with Christians but also with each other. This holds out tremendous promise for the future, for we are only at the beginning of the movement.

But of course we must not allow ourselves to forget that we visited only the most beautiful areas and did so in the springtime, a time which transfigures everything or, to use another image, we made our visit in the fresh experience of a honeymoon. In this very same Asia there are also immense waste landscapes where sand and stones and lack of rain make life hard for every sort of creature. This too belongs to the full reality which one must know about.

In other words, in this book we have presented only one side of the coin; it is a true one and has to be taken seriously. And we also have to be aware that not all christian theologians share these new insights and interpretations any more than all non-christians go along with this new departure. As well as legitimate and tolerant theological pluralism there are also people set in their ways, belligerent nests of resistance, who use all the weapons they have and their deepest convictions to proceed against the new theology. In a book which was even handed to the Council Fathers in autumn 1965, H. van Straelen claims that there is a tragic trench between the missionaries and K. Rahner and like-minded theologians. The professors, he claims, do their theologising in the clouds, while the missionaries live side by side with these religions and see them in a less ideal way. He regrets also, that in Holland and Germany, individual churches, including even Cologne Cathedral, have been placed at the disposal of the Muslims for their religious meetings — a parish hall would have been more than sufficient. Finally, he attacks the "doctrine of salvationitis" which, he says, bears the main blame for the easing-off of missionary zeal[97] (cf. also what was said at the end of Chapter 5).

Theologians of this type have their function in the

Church, provided that they do not immediately make their opinions into an article of faith. Both in Scripture and in Tradition the religions do in fact always appear in a peculiar double light. Good things and bad things are said about them, they are seen as light and as darkness, as ways of salvation and of damnation. At the point at which they contact Christianity one sees continuity and discontinuity. The emphasis placed on one or other side has varied according to times and mentalities. Nowadays, looking at the one world and one human race, we rightly concentrate rather on the positive aspects; this being so, others are justified in pointing out the negative aspects to prevent us all too easily making certainty of salvation out of hope of salvation.

The only condition is that these voices should not become fanatical and primitive, as happens among the "Catholic Traditionalists". These people fight against the "aberrations" of the second Vatican Council, and on our present topic of the non-christian religions they nail down the "traditional teaching" in the following way: "Original sin, the source of all other sins, is thus the source also of all pagan 'religions' as schismatic, heretical, apostate distortions, mutilations, abbreviations and counterfeits of the one true religion. Hence they are all symptoms of opposition to God, of untruthfulness, stupidity and help-lessness; they are under the dominion of Satan, the father of sin which is expressed at one time in objective dis-orientation, at another in the modal adulteration of religion and sometimes in both ways at once. Thus the 'religions' are the 'selfish', that is, self-willed, self-initiated and therefore misleading and ineffectual ways to which God left the human race after the first sin (Acts 14, 16)".[98]

We must become aware of the other side of reality not only on the theological plane but also in the concrete situation. It would be quite wrong to think that the whole world of the Asiatic religions is flirting with Christianity and walking along holding hands with it. In Chapter 12 we spoke about the peculiar love-hate relationship between Christianity and Islam in Indonesia. There and elsewhere time and again volcano-like eruptions take place. For instance, Muhammad Rasjidi, Professor of Islamology at the University of Jakarta and therefore an educated man, is a typical representative of the fanatical wing. At an inter-religious meeting of the WCC held in Karachi in 1976 at which christian mission and muslim witness were discussed, he put forward 13 charges against the Christians in Indonesia. Among these were: the Christians receive a lot of money from abroad with which they buy land in all the villages and in the best parts of the towns and build their triumphalistic churches; they distribute food and clothing and in this way entice the poor; they bring the school-children into contact with pen-friends, who give them presents, thus winning them for the Church; the children and young people are offered films and entertainments; through the western secularisation which the Churches promote the identity of the Muslims is destroyed. Rasjidi speaks frankly about religious aggression and the spiritual exploitation of the weak by the strong, which is made worse, he says, by the fact that this takes place in the name of religion.[99]

But exactly the same things and even worse things are said about the Muslims in different countries; that they are using government money or dollars gained from Arabian oil to build mosques and are pushing the christian minorities on one side. A recent report describes the Muslims in the Philippines as having a crusading attitude towards the Christians, in Indonesia one of rivalry and in Malaysia one of apartheid.[100] Some experts in this field assert that Islam from its very nature must behave in a belligerent way, that it regards itself as the last and only legitimate religion, that it divides the world up into muslim countries and enemy countries and that the most it can do is to permit a tactical truce but never a firm peace.[101]

We can see how a lot on both sides is not yet "up to date". In the past 20 years a lot has changed for the better, but both at the top and at grass-roots level much formation of consciousness has to take place, so that the whole people can set out along the new way. Those religions are in the position we were in until recently — they are in the "Middle Ages" and have ways of thought and attitudes which we today regard as outdated. They have no leading figures like John XXIII, no documents like *Pacem in terris* or *Gaudium et spes*. In spite of this we are aware of the motive power of ideas. It has always been the case that the thoughts of the élite came down to the ordinary folk. Which is why all the discussions and meetings we have mentioned — and those we have not mentioned — have their point; they mark out the way for the future. In christian circles, too, a lot of educative work still needs to be done in order to demolish set positions so that the missionaries accept dialogue as the new attitude and do not feel betrayed by theology as some claim.

At the beginning of these 20 years when we realised the reality of religious pluralism and became conscious of the strength in spirit and in numbers of those religions, we experienced this as a great trial and test of faith. So much of our position of monopoly was relativised and lowered. As Christians we lost something in the way of alleged privileges, but as religious people we gained enormously. Christ and God's plan of salvation now appears greater, more divine. And so we grow too and are able to walk into the world's horizon freely and with quickened step. Young Christians can be won back to a vision like this, for they naturally, and out of a divine instinct, are unsympathetic towards all privileges and monopolies.

But what, you may ask, about the danger of syncretism, that unchristian medley of all religions? This danger exists and must be taken seriously. One person who could speak from experience was M. W. Visser't Hooft, former General Secretary of the WCC; he warned of this danger in an urgent appeal.[102] The only appropriate way to overcome this danger is through a strengthening of faith in the central happening of christian revelation and not through a fresh isolation. Nowadays we know better than we did before how Israel's religion was interspersed with many religious elements taken from the neighbouring peoples and yet asserted itself as a monotheistic religion. "The integration of the fathers' religion through the basic writings of the Pentateuch belongs to the boldest efforts of the religious thinking of humankind. The polytheism of the age of the patriarchs is not condemned and rejected as such, but is overlaid and assimilated as a prelude to, a pledge of primitive history of the religion of Yahweh. The interpreters of primitive history are aware from their deeper knowledge of the living God that the same living God 'spoke in many and various ways to the fathers' (Heb 1:1). That was true religion coming into being".[103] All contact with other religions must be forbidden only to immature Christians and it is only timorous Church leaders who see all concrete steps towards the incarnation of theology and liturgy in the other cultures as like the dangers of syncretism and of all heresies. Not narrow measures but greater faith in Christ and in his Spirit build the right defence against false influences from those religions.

Certain influences, of course, we ought to allow to permeate, for these will be beneficial not harmful. We are right to present Christianity as the fulfilment of the non-christian religions, but to a certain degree this fulfilment ought to be understood as something mutual. This does not mean that we expect an angel to come down from heaven and bring us another revelation (cf. Gal 1:8). But some of their values, experiences, techniques of meditation which we have not developed to the same degree can help us "to grow in the knowledge of our Lord Jesus Christ" (2 Pet 3:18). Can Asia perhaps even help us, who over the centuries have painted over Christ with so many theological formulae and colours, to discover him once again in his unadulterated originality? M. Mildenberger concludes his book *Heil aus Asien?* ("Salvation from Asia?") with a reflection along these lines. He says: "Finally, here and there, there is beginning to emerge, even though vaguely and in embryonic form, something which moves one in a peculiar way, viz. that Asia which, with its own religious qualities, is coming into the post-christian West, is bringing Jesus Christ back to the West. ... People are asking hesitatingly, gropingly and sometimes with great happiness once again for Jesus Christ. This Jesus who is found here is different from the Jesus of conventional Christianity; he is, as it were, a 'meditative' Jesus, who has the characteristics of St John's Gospel. This is how many Buddhists and Hindus have understood him, and they are asking about him and his spirituality".[104]

On the journey along the road to the religions, not only have the ranks of Christians drawn closer together, but all religious people feel more united and more courageous in the midst of a world which no longer believes. As recently as five years ago the final word about God seemed to be that he was dead and that the wave of secularisation could not be halted in its triumphal progress through the world. Since then we have already got round again to talking with new hope about mysticism and the experience of God.

The French Revolution made the democratic rights of liberty, equality and fraternity acceptable and the socialist revolution won rights for the workers. Now there seems to be a third revolution sweeping through the world, a revolution which is making religious values once again accepted as normal in the eyes of the world at large; and the tragedy is that these values were declared by Christians to be a "private affair" of which they were almost ashamed. In this third revolution the coloured, non-christian peoples are playing their great rôle. This is the work of the Spirit, who really does "fill the whole earth" as we sing at Pentecost!

The groups of Marxists and secularists smile at new hopes of this kind, for in their view the crisis of Christianity is a terminal one, since religion is destined for extinction in the world of science. Now, if Christianity is bound to succumb to the virus of secularisation, how much more certainly will not the other religions succumb even though Christianity may predecease them by some time: omittance is not acquittance. This is why, they say, to occupy oneself with the world religions is "a backward-looking business in view of the twilight of the gods which is taking place everywhere; in other words, it is a romantic anachronism".[105]

This is a question of life and death. Two concepts of life — those of faith and ideology — rebound against each other with great force as regards this question. The chances of any sort of reconciliation are slim. We can only let both these viewpoints remain as they are and say that we will talk about them again in 50 years' time. For even if faith, against all evidence shown, holds fast to its message, in our case, facts shown by experience can support it. In the most secularised country of the world, Japan of all places, a number of new religions have sprung up; there has been a resurge of religious activity with common prayer, singing and bible study amongst religious young people in particular, who had previously been "written-off"; in Russia, after 60 years of Communism and struggles, a religious life has been aroused among the youth and the intellectuals.[106]

For our part, we believe that when secularism has swept away all the clouds and has failed to find a weather-God behind them, it will be plain to see that only an unfathomable blue mass remains, something which even for the astronauts has no end. In other words, the human person will always be small and restless, but open towards the infinite, until he has penetrated the mystery and has found God. He will never get ahead of his own shadow, he will never be able to free himself from this religious question. It constitutes a part of his humanity. He can abandon churches and religions, institutions and structures. Yet without being aware of it he will become a religious nomad, who does not so much *know* his way and answer to the meaning of his life, but more so one who *strives* to seek the answer. Since he is a human being and not an animal, and recognises his existence, he asks the whys and wherefores. Since he discovers himself in all the different situations in his life: in sickness, misfortune, death, even in the highlights of his life, ecstatic joy, which is never complete or lasting, he asks himself: Is this all that life offers? He feels the emptiness and the frustration. He can persuade himself that there is no answer to these questions. And yet his heart is continually bursting with this question. He therefore has the choice either to accept the ultimate meaning of life or to surrender himself to total absurdity. At present, however, despite everything, life is good and worth living, and — for the time being — it offers so many meaningful alternatives, that it will also solve the ultimate question of life in an explicit way, in other words, worldly life is evidently embedded in the ultimate question of life.

Yet whoever constantly remains in the dark side or fearful side of life has an even greater claim to a final compromise.

The mystery of all the religions flows through the mystery of a faith, then through the mystery of a person who lives the religion, into the mystery of Man. Each individual chooses his own path. Jesus Christ assured us of a foundation to life, which we call "Father in heaven". Whoever accepts this interpretation has certainly not made a bad choice.

If this explanation is to be taken seriously, it already provides the soul with confidence, and helps us to fight "regardlessly" for a more just world, that is to say, to fight without fear of opposition and danger.

NOTES

[1] H. R. Weber, "Gottes Arithmetik in der Mission", in *Kirchentreu und Kirchenfern*, Wuppertal, 1967, 63-73. D. Barrett, "A.D. 2000! 350 million Christians in Africa", in *International Review of Mission*, Geneva, 1970, 39-54.

[2] T. Ohm, *Asiens Nein und Ja*, 214.

[3] G. Schurhammer, Franz Xaver II/I, 1-130.

[4] A. Goodier, *Saints for Sinners. The failure of St Francis Xavier*, London, 1936. J. Brodrick, *Abenteuer Gottes*, Stuttgart, 1954.

[5] J. Brodrick, op. cit., 279, 306, 427.

[6] W. Bühlmann, *Pionier der Einheit. Anastasius Hartmann*, Zurich, 1966, 64ff, 143-147, 218ff, 227-230.

[7] W. Bühlmann, op. cit., 54, 70.

[8] J. Beckmann, *Die katholische Missionsmethode in China neuester Zeit*, Immensee, 1931, 42. Same author: "Die Stellung der katholischen Missionare zur chines. Kultur", in *Katholisches Missionsjahrbuch der Schweiz*, Freiburg, 1942, 41-67.

[9] *Méthode de l'apostolat moderne en Chine*, Hong Kong, 1911.

[10] J. Beckmann, *Weltkirche und Weltreligionen*, 17.

[11] T. Ohm, op. cit., 177-192. For a similar situation in Africa see W. Bühlmann, *Missionsprozess in Addis Abeba*, Frankfurt a.M., 1977. English translation, *The Missions on Trial*, Slough/New York, 1978.

[12] op. cit., 184.

[13] Die Liebe Gottes in den nichtchristlichen Religionen 442, 389ff.

[14] J. Jesudasan, "Gandhian perspectives on missiology", in *Indian Church History Review* 4 (Mysore, 1970), 45-72, esp. 63ff, 66ff.

[15] J. Auf der Maur, "Kirchliche Verlautbarungen über die nichtchristlichen Religionen", in *Katholisches Missionsjahrbuch der Schweiz*, Freiburg, 1966, 31-43.

[16] W. Henkel, *Die religiöse Situation der Heiden*, 209ff, 54ff, 111ff.

[17] Das Religiöse in der Menschheit und das Christentum.

[18] op. cit., Foreword.

[19] G. Caprile, *Il Concilio*, III, 313.

[20] G. Caprile, op. cit., IV, 84.

[21] K. Rahner and H. Vorgrimmler, *Kleines Konzilskompendium*, Freiburg i.B., 1966, 350.

[22] G. Caprile, op. cit., III, 460-466.

[23] In *L'Osservatore Romano*, 25th-26th November, 1963.

[24] G. Caprile, op. cit., II, 415ff, 500; III, 366. R. M. Wiltgen, *The Rhine flows into the Tiber*, New York, 1967, 73-78.

[25] Approche du non-chrétien, XXXIV *Semaine de Missiologie de Louvain*, 1964. Le Missioni e le Religioni non cristiane, *Quinta Settimana di Studi missionari*, Milano, 1964.

[26] L. Wiedenmann, "Wallfahrt nach Bombay. Eindrücke zum 38. Eucharistischen Kongress", in *Kathol. Missionen*, Bonn, 1965, 39-44; *38th International Eucharistic Congress Bombay 1964*, 2 vols., Bombay, 1965.

213

[27] *L'Osservatore Romano*, 4th December, 1964.

[28] The editor of the journal *Le Christ au Monde* published in several languages in Rome in which a long feud against this theology was carried out.

[29] See his book in the Bibliography. See his criticism on the Bombay Congress in *Bulletin Saint-Jean-Baptiste*, January, 1965, 103-105. For an answer, see J. Masson, "Face aux religions non chretiennes", in *Spiritus* 25 (Paris, 1965), 416-425.

[30] All the lectures in J. Neuner, *Christian revelation*. In addition: H. Küng, *Christenheit als Minderheit*.

[31] S. Samartha, "Dialogue between men of living faiths"; Margull-Samartha, "Dialog mit den andern Religionen"; K. Klostermann, "Dialog der Weltreligionen". Zur ökumenischen Studienkonferenz in Beirut, in *Kathol. Missionen* 1970, 120-124.

[32] W. Bühlmann, "Die Theologie der nichtchristlichen Religionen als ökumenisches Problem", in *Freiheit in der Begegnung*. Commemorative publication, O. Karrer, Frankfurt a.M., 1969, 453-478.

[33] A more extensive coverage can be found in W. Bühlmann, op. cit.

[34] See Margull-Samartha, op. cit., 165-178.

[35] See the list in *Minutes of the Second Meeting of the Working Group*, New Delhi, September 1974, Geneva, 37ff.

[36] See the corresponding reports in *Bulletin of the Secretariat for non-Christians*.

[37] W. Jentsch, *Evangelischer Erwachsenenkatechismus*, Kursbuch des Glaubens, Gütersloh, 1975, 1226.

[38] M. S. Abdullah, "Ein Bericht über die Haltung der islamischen Weltorganisationen zum Dialog und Trialog", in *Kathol. Missionen* 1976, 163-167. In addition, *Kathol. Missionen* 1973, 76. The same author in *Ständige Arbeitsgruppe, Christen und Moslems*, 66-73.

[39] M. A. Lücker (ed.), *Religionen, Frieden und Menschenrechte*. The same author, "Friedenskonferenz der Weltreligionen", in *Kathol. Missionen* 1971, 50-52.

[40] Report, *World religions and peace*, Boston, 1968.

[41] See the news in *Informationen*, Weltkonferenz der Religionen für den Frieden, Bismarckstrasse 25, 5300 Bonn; Religion for Peace, *Newsletter*, 777 United Nations Plaza, New York, N.Y., 10017 USA.

[42] The visit of His Holiness Pope Paul VI to the Philippines and the Asian Bishops' Meeting, Manila, 1971, 234-237, 238.

[43] op. cit., 112ff, 53-57, 97ff.

[44] This statement first caused a sensation in H. Halbfass's *Fundamentalkatechtik*, Düsseldorf, 1968.

[45] J. Pathrapankal, *Service and salvation*; M. Dhavamony, *Evangelisation* (see Bibliography); M. Lederle, "Theologen stellen sich den Missionaren. Bericht über eine internationale Theologenkonferenz in Nagpur", in *Kathol. Missionen* 1972, 8-12.

[46] Church in India today. All India Seminar, Bangalore, 1969. New Delhi (s.a.), 339-343, 244.

[47] D. S. Amalorpavadass, *Research Seminar*.

[48] J. Dupuis, "Planning the liturgy tomorrow", in *Clergy Monthly* 1972, 93-105.

[49] This is J. Neuner's opinion in "Heilige Bücher der Weltreligionen in der Liturgie?" in *Kathol. Missionen* 1975, 45-48.

[50] *Concilium* n. 112, 1976, Italian edition 12 (1976), fasc. 2.

[51] See S.C. de Propaganda Fide memoria rerum, Freiburg i.B., 1972, I/1, 592-595; II, 938. In addition, Malcolm Hay, *The failure in the Far East*, Wetteren, 1956.

[52] K. Rahner, Uber die Schrift-Inspiration, *Quaestiones Disputatae*, Freiburg i.B., 1958, 85.

[53] See the report on the meeting by J. N. Kuruchi in *Bulletin of the Secretariat for non-Christians*, 1973, 68-72.

[54] See Bibliography under C.B.C.I.

[55] L. Iriarte, "Die missionarisch-franziskanische Spiritualität", in Plenarrat des Kapuzinerordens 1978, 1-13.

[56] Various authors, *Les moines chrétiens*, 359ff.

[57] Missionszentrale der Franziskaner, *Dialogue with Asian religions*.

[58] M. R. M. Muskens, *Partner beim Aufbau. Die katholische Kirche in Indonesien*, Aachen, 1978; PMV Bulletin, Brussels, 1977/64: *Indonésie;* U. Beyer, *Entwicklung im Paradies*, Frankfurt a.M., 1974.

[59] S. Samartha, *Dialogue* 75-80.

[60] I am grateful to M.R.M. Muskens for this latest information. He took part in the People's Congress as an observer.

[61] See *China News Analysis*, Weekly newsletters, Hong Kong, 4th November, 1977.

[62] PMV Bulletin, Le coloque de Louvain; Various authors, *Christian faith*.

[63] P. Hebblethwaite, *Mehr Christentum oder mehr Marxismus?* Frankfurt a.M., 1977, 123-147; Christian-Marxist Dialogue and Beyond, London, 1977.

[64] A. Lazzarotto, *Esperienza cinese*.

[65] See J. Delaney, *A report on a survey of religious women in Hong Kong*, Hong Kong, 1975; Diocese of Hong Kong, *A report on a survey of priests and brothers*, Hong Kong, 1977. These show that a lot of questions are being asked about the future and a new kind of existence, but the actual problem of China is dealt with to a very small extent only.

[66] Ch. McCarthy, "Le Filippine e l'evangelizzazione dell'Asia", in *La Civiltà Cattolica*, Rome, 1970, 360-369.

[67] Ch. McCarthy, op. cit.; PMV Bulletin, Brussels, 1970/30; M. A. Bernad, *The christianization of the Philippines*, Manila, 1970.

[68] A. Guerrero, *Philippine society and revolution*, Manila, 1971, esp. 184-194, 296.

[69] *Acta Apostolicae Sedis* 1971, 922.

[70] See B. A. Mayo, "Some reflections on religious experiences in the Philippines", in *National Conference of Major Religious Superiors of Australia*, Wahroonga, 1977, 1-25; PMV-Dossier, May-June 1977.

[71] For example in *Vaterland*, Lucerne, 17th February, 1978.

[72] Printed in *Dialogue*, n. 22, October 1970.

[73] See, for example, B. J. Rich, *Life together in small christian communities*. A leadership training course, Davao City, 1977. Basic christian community Series. The Cardinal Bea Institute, Box 4082, Manila.

[74] P. François-Régis du Lascuet, *La trouée. Le Père Charles*, Paris, 1947.

[75] J. Dournes, *Dieu aime les païens*, Paris, 1963.

[76] See the six books by J. Sinclair. In addition, N. Gash and J. Whittacker, *A pictorial history of New Guinea*, Hong Kong, 1975; R. M. Glasse, *Huli of Papua*, Paris-The Hague, 1968.

[77] *Bulletin of the Secretariat for non-Christians*, 1976, 337-340; ibid., 1977, 191ff.

[78] This standing working party published the book *Christen und Moslems in Deutschland*, Essen, 1977.

[79] K. Hoppenworth, *Islam contra Christentum - gestern und heute*, Bad Liebezell, 1976; K. Hutten and S. von Kortzfleish (eds.), *Asien missioniert im Abendland*, Stuttgart, 1962; G. V. Vicedom, *Die Weltreligionen im Angriff auf die Christenheit*, Munich, 1957.

[80] Klages-Heutger, "Weltreligionen und Christentum im Gespräch"; Mildenberger, "Heil aus Asien?"; H. Küng, "Die Herausforderung der Weltreligionen", in *Christein*, Munich, 1974, 81-108.

[81] M. Mildenberger, op. cit., 88.

[82] See J. Mattam, *Land of the Trinity*, 74, 183-185.

[83] K. Klostermaier, *Hinduismus*, 407.

[84] P. Rossano, *Il problema teologico*, 27ff.

[85] See M. Peitz, *Die Hoffnung der Völker*, 37ff.

[86] *Bulletin of the Secretariat for non-Christians*, 12 (1977), 140ff; S. Samartha, *Faith in the midst of faiths*.

[87] *L'Osservatore Romano*, 28th June, 1964.

[88] For some additional information see P. Meinhold, *Die Religionen der Gegenwart*, 49-68.

[89] *Summa theologica*, II-II, q 2, a 2, ad 3.

[90] In addition to the texts used in Chapter 9, see also G. Thils, *Syncrétisme*, 38-48; P. Rossano, "Y-a-t-il une révélation authentique en dehors de la révélation judéo-chrétienne?", in *Bulletin of the Secretariat for non-Christians*, 1968/8, 82-84; Studia Missionalia, *Revelation in Christianity and other religions*, Rome, 1971; Ishanand Vempeny, *Inspiration in the non-biblical scriptures*, Bangalore, 1973. Various authors, cf. Bibliography.

[91] K. Rahner, "Das Christentum und die nichtchristlichen Religionen"; J. Feiner, "Kirche und Heilsgeschichte", in *Gott in Welt*, Festschrift K. Rahner II, 317-345. See also the contributions by J. Ratzinger and H. R. Schlette in this commemorative publication. G. Thils, op. cit., 48-58.

[92] S. Regli, "Uberlegungen zum Absolutheitsanspruch des Christentums", in *Wissenschaft und Weisheit*, Mönchengladbach, 1977, 100-124, esp. 122ff; Kasper, *Absolutheit*.

[93] Regula non bullata, cap. 16.

[94] J. A. Cuttat, *Asiatische Gottheit*, 224.

[95] See the different books by J. B. Metz, for example, *Zur Theologie der welt*, Munich, 1969.

[96] M. Mildenberger, *Heil aus Asien?* 91.

[97] H. van Straelen, *Our attitude towards other religions*, Tokyo, 1965, 25ff, 79, 106ff. The same author, *The Catholic encounter with world religions*, London, 1966. L. Elders wrote similar things in various

journals, e.g., "Die Taufe der Weltreligionen", in *Theologie und Glaube* 55 (1965), 124-131.

[98] A. Holzer, *Vaticanum II*, Basel, 1977, 179ff. Published by the Union of loyal Catholics in Switzerland.

[99] The whole of n. 260 of the *International Review of Mission*, Geneva, 1976, esp. 427-438.

[100] P. G. Gowin, "Past and present postures in Christian-Muslim relationships in Insular South East Asia", in *The South East Asia Journal of Theology*, 18 (1977), 38-54.

[101] As, for example, Paul Bassim Hakkim, Vicar apostolic of Beirut, in a report to the Secretariat for the non-Christian religions in Rome, July 1977.

[102] M. Visser't Hooft, *L'église face au syncrétisme. La tentation du mélange religieux*, Geneva, 1964; T. Yamamari and Ch. Taker, *Christopaganism or indigenous Christianity?*, South Pasadena, 1975. See Thil's answer to this in *Syncrétisme ou catholicité?*

[103] H. U. von Balthasar, in *Mysterium salutis* II, 42. See also H. Waldenfels, "Zur Heilsbedeutung der nichtchristlichen Religionen in katholischer Sicht", in *Zeitschrift für Missionswissenschaft und Religionswissenschaft*, 1969, 257-278.

[104] M. Mildenberger, *Heil aus dem Osten?*, 98ff.

[105] So G. Rothermund quotes in G. Klages, *Weltreligionen*, 27.

[106] H. B. Earhart, *The new religions of Japan*, Tokyo, 1970; E. Benz, *Neue Religionen*, Stuttgart, 1971; H. Biezais (ed.), *New religions*, Stockholm, 1975; P. Meinzold, *Aussenseiter der Kirchen. Was wollen die modernen Erneuerungsbewegungen?*, Freiburg i.B., 1976.

BIBLIOGRAPHY

The numerous general books on religions and individual religions are not listed here. Only those which portray the encounter of the religions with Christianity are quoted.

Ancilli, E., (ed.), *La mistica non cristiana*, Brescia, 1969.
Anderson, J. N. D., *Jesus, Krishna, Mohammed. Christentum und Weltreligionen in Auseinandersetzung*, Wuppertal, 1972. (*Christianity and comparative religion*, London, 1972).
Amalorpavadass, D. S. (ed.), *Research Seminar on non-biblical scriptures*, Bangalore, 1975.
Balchand, A., *The salvific value of non-christian religions according to Asian christian theologians*, Manila, 1973.
Basetti Sani, G., *Il Corano nella luce di Cristo*, Verona, 1972.
Beckmann, J., *Weltkirche und Weltreligionen*, Freiburg i.B., 1960.
Benz, E. - Nambara, M., *Das Christentum und die nichtchristlichen Hochreligionen*. Eine internationale Bibliographie, Leiden, 1960.
Boublik, V., *Teologia delle religioni*, Rome, 1973.
Brown, D. A., *A guide to religions*, London, 1975.
Brodrick, J., *Abenteurer Gottes. Leben und Fahrten des heiligen Franz Xaver*, Stuttgart, 1959. (Saint Francis Xavier, London, 1952.)
Bulletin, *Secretariatus pro non christianis*, Rome, 1966ff.
Camps, A., *Christendom en godsdiensten der wereld*, Baarn, 1976.
— *De Weg, de paden en de wegen*, Baarn, 1977.
Caprile, G., *Il Concilio Vaticano II*, V vol., Rome, 1965/69.
C.B.C.I. Dialogue Commission, *Guidelines for inter-religious dialogue*, Varanasi, 1977.
Cornelis, E., *Valeurs chrétiennes des religions non-chrétiennes*, Paris, 1965.
Cragg, Kenneth, *Alive to God. Muslim and Christian prayer*, London, 1970.
Cuttat, J. A., *Le dialogue spirituel Orient-Occident*, Louvain, 1964.
Daniélou, J., *Vom Heil der Völker*, Frankfurt a.M., 1952.
Dhavamony, M. (ed.), *Evangelization, dialogue and development*. International Theological Conference Nagpur, Rome, 1972.
Dialogue, Colombo, 1974ff.
Dournes, J., *Gott liebt die Heiden*, Freiburg i.B., 1966. (Dieu aime les païens, Lyon, 1963.)
— *L'offrande des peuples*, Paris, 1967.
Dumoulin, H., *Christlicher Dialog mit Asien*, Munich, 1970.
— *Christianity meets Buddhism*, La Salle, Illinois, 1974.
Evers, G., *Mission, nichtchristliche Welt, weltliche Welt*, Münster, 1974.
Falaturi, A., Petuchowski, J., Strolz, W. (eds.), *Drei Wege zu dem einen Gott. Glaubenserfahrung in den monotheistischen Religionen*, Freiburg i.B., 1976.
Fitzgerald, M. (ed.), *Moslems und Christen - Partner?*, Graz, 1976.
Friedli, R., *Fremdheit als Heimat. Auf der Suche nach einem Kriterium für den Dialog zwischen den Religionen*, Freiburg CH, 1974.
Duraisingh, Ch., Hargreaves, C. (eds.), *India's search for reality and the relevance of the gospel of John*, Delhi, 1975.

Heilbetz, *Theologische Gründe der nichtchristlichen Religionen*, Freiburg i.B., 1967.

Henkel, W., *Die religiöse Situation der Heiden und ihre Bekehrung nach J. H. Newman*, Rome, 1967.

Ishanand Vempeny, *Inspiration in the non-biblical scriptures*, Bangalore, 1973.

Karrer, O., *Das Religiöse in der Menscheit und das Christentum*, Freiburg i.B., 1934.

Kerkhofs, J., Henry, A. M. (eds.), *Dialogue d'aujourd'hui - Mission de demain*, Paris, 1968.

King, W. L., *Buddhism and Christianity. Some bridges of understanding*, London, 1962.

Klages, G., Heutger, N., *Weltreligionen und Christentum im Gespräch. Die Weltreligionen im Unterricht*, Hildesheim-New York, 1977.

Klinger, E. (ed.), *Christentum innerhalb und ausserhalb der Kirche*, Freiburg i.B., 1976.

Kostermaier, K., *Hinduismus*, Cologne, 1965.

König, F., *Christus und die Religionen der Erde*, 3rd vol., Freiburg i.B., 1951.

Küng, H., *Christenheit als Minderheit. Die Kirche unter den Weltreligionen*, Einsiedeln, 1965.

Kunnumpuram, K., *Ways of salvation. The salvific meaning of non-christian religions according to the teaching of Vatican II*, Poona, 1971.

Lazzarotto, A. (ed.), *Esperienza cinese e fede cristiana*, Bologna, 1976.

Le Saux, *Sagesse hindoue, Mystique chrétienne*, Paris, 1965. (*Indische Weisheit, christliche Mystik*, Lucerne, 1968.)

Lücker, M. (ed.), *Religionen, Frieden, Menschenrechte*. Dokumentation der ersten Weltkonferenz der Religionen für den Frieden in Kyoto 1970, Wuppertal, 1971.

Lynn A. de Silva, *Of the self in Buddhism and Christianity*, Colombo, 1975.

Margull, H. J., Samartha, S. J. (eds.), *Dialog mit den anderen Religionen. Material aus der ökumenischen Bewegung*, Frankfurt a.M., 1972.

Mattam, J., *Land of the Trinity. A study on modern christian approaches to Hinduism*, Bangalore, 1975.

Meinhold, P., *Die Religionen der Gegenwart*, Freiburg i.B., 1978.

Mensching, G., *Der offene Tempel. Die Weltreligionen im Gespräch miteinander*, Stuttgart, 1974.

Mildenberger, M., *Heil aus Asien? Hinduistische und buddhistische Bewegungen im Westen*, Stuttgart, 1974.

Molinski, W. (ed.), *Die vielen Wege zum Heil. Heilsanspruch und Heilsbedeutung der nichtchristlichen Religionen*, Munich, 1969.

Müller, K., *Die Kirche und die nichtchristlichen Religionen*, Aschaffenburg, 1968.

Neuner, J. (ed.), *Hinduismus und Christentum*, Vienna, 1962.

— *Christian revelation and world religions*, London, 1967.

Nys, H., *Le salut sans l'Evangile*, Paris, 1966.

Ohm, T., *Die Liebe zu Gott in den nichtchristlichen Religionen*, Munich, 1950.

— *Asiens Nein und Ja zum westlichen Christentum*, Munich, 1960.
— *Mohammedaner und Katholiken*, Munich, 1961.
Pathrapankal, J. (ed.), *Service and salvation*. Theological Conference on Evangelization at Nagpur, Bangalore, 1973.
Panikkar, R., *The unknown Christ of Hinduism*, London, 1964. (*Christus, der Unbekannte im Hinduismus*, Lucerne, 1965.)
— *Religionen und die Religion*, Munich, 1965.
Peitz, M., *Wenn wir weiterleben wollen. Welbekenntnisse antworten auf Probleme unserer Zeit*, Munich, 1972.
— *Die Hoffnung der Völker. Berichte und Portraits aus der Kirche in Asien*, Düsseldorf, 1976.
PMV Bulletin, *Le colloque de Louvain sur la Chine*, Brussels, 1974, n. 54.
Rahner, K., "Das Christentum und die nichtchristlichen Religionen", in *Schriften zur Theologie V*, Einsiedeln, 1962, (136-158).
Rahner, H., Ratzinger, J., *Das Christentum und die nichtchristlichen Religionen*, Nuremberg, 1965.
Rosenkranz, G., *Religionswissenschaft und Theologie*, Munich, 1964.
Rossano, P., *Il problema teologico delle religioni*, Rome, 1975.
Samartha, S., *Hindus vor dem universalen Christus*, Stuttgart, 1970.
— (ed.), *Dialogue between men of living faiths*. Papers presented at a consultation held at Ajaltoun, Lebanon; Geneva, 1971.
— (ed.), *Faith in the midst of faiths. Consultation of Chiang Mai on dialogue in community*, Geneva, 1977.
Schlette, H. R., *Die Religionen als Thema der Theologie*, Freiburg i.B., 1964.
Schurhammer, G., *Franz Xaver. Seine Leben und seine Zeit*, 2 vols., Freiburg i.B., 1955/1973.
Secretariatus pro non christianis, *Religions*, Rome, 1970.
— *A la rencontre des religions africaines*, Rome, 1968.
Siegmund, G., *Buddhismus und Christentum*, Frankfurt a.M., 1968.
Ständige Arbeitsgruppe für christlich-islamische Beziehungen und für Kontakte zu andern Weltreligionen. *Christen und Moslems in Deutschland*, Essen, 1977.
Thils, G., *Propos et problèmes de la théologie des religions non chrétiennes*, Casterman, 1966.
— *Syncrétisme ou catholicité?*, Paris, 1967.
Various authors, *Offenbarung*. Symposium über den Begriff der Offenbarung, Vienna, 1974.
— *Les moines chrétiens face aux religions d'Asie*, Vanves, 1974.
— *Revelation in christianity and other religions*, Studia missionalia, Rome, 1971.
— *Thema Weltreligionen*. Ein Diskussions - und Arbeitsbuch für Religionspädagogen und Religionswissenschaftler, Munich, 1977.
Waldenfels, H., *Absolutes Nichts*. Zur Grundlegung des Dialoges zwischen Buddhismus und Christentum, Freiburg i.B., 1976.
Welte, P. H., *Die Heilsbedürftigkeit des Menschen*, Freiburg i.B., 1976.
Zaehner, R. C., *Inde, Israel, Islam religions mystiques et révélations prophétiques*, Desclée de Brouwer, 1965.

Other Orbis books . . .

THE MEANING OF MISSION
José Comblin

"This very readable book has made me think, and I feel it will be useful for anyone dealing with their Christian role of mission and evangelism." *New Review of Books and Religion*
ISBN 0-88344-304-X CIP   *Cloth $6.95*

THE GOSPEL OF PEACE AND JUSTICE
Catholic Social Teaching Since Pope John

Presented by Joseph Gremillion

"Especially valuable as a resource. The book brings together 22 documents containing the developing social teaching of the church from *Mater et Magistra* to Pope Paul's 1975 *Peace Day Message on Reconciliation*. I watched the intellectual excitement of students who used Gremillion's book in a justice and peace course I taught last summer, as they discovered a body of teaching on the issues they had defined as relevant. To read Gremillion's overview and prospectus, a meaty introductory essay of some 140 pages, is to be guided through the sea of social teaching by a remarkably adept navigator."
National Catholic Reporter
    "An authoritative guide and study aid for concerned Catholics and others." *Library Journal*
ISBN 0-88344-165-9   *Cloth $15.95*
ISBN 0-88344-166-7   *Paper $8.95*

THEOLOGY IN THE AMERICAS
Papers of the 1975 Detroit Conference

Edited by Sergio Torres and John Eagleson

"A pathbreaking book from and about a pathbreaking theological conference, *Theology in the Americas* makes a major contribution to ecumenical theology, Christian social ethics and liberation movements in dialogue." *Fellowship*
ISBN 0-88344-479-8 CIP   *Cloth $12.95*
ISBN 0-88344-476-3   *Paper $5.95*

LOVE AN
IN MAO'S

BR127 .B7613 19 0   c.1
Buhlmann, Walbe t. c   100105 000
The search for Go d : an encou

3 9310 00039160 5
GOSHEN COLLEGE-GOOD LIBRARY

Raymond L

"Mao's tho   reassess his own
philosophy   Christian. His well
documented and meticulously expounded philosophy of Mao's love
and struggle-thought might do as much for many a searching
reader." *Prairie Messenger*
ISBN 0-88344-289-2 CIP   *Cloth $8.95*
ISBN 0-88344-290-6   *Paper $3.95*

WATERBUFFALO THEOLOGY

Kosuke Koyama

"This book with its vivid metaphors, fresh imagination and creative
symbolism is a 'must' for anyone desiring to gain a glimpse into the
Asian mind." *Evangelical Missions Quarterly*
ISBN 0-88344-702-9   *Paper $4.95*

ASIAN VOICES
IN CHRISTIAN THEOLOGY

Edited by Gerald H. Anderson

"A basic sourcebook for anyone interested in the state of Protestant
theology in Asia today. I am aware of no other book in English that
treats this matter more completely." *National Catholic Reporter*
ISBN 0-88344-017-2   *Cloth $15.00*
ISBN 0-88344-016-4   *Paper $7.95*

FAREWELL TO INNOCENCE

Allan Boesak

"This is an extremely helpful book. The treatment of the themes of
power, liberation, and reconciliation is precise, original, and
Biblically-rooted. Dr. Boesak has done much to advance the discussion, and no one who is interested in these matters can afford to
ignore his important contribution." *Richard J. Mouw, Calvin College*
ISBN 0-88344-130-6 CIP   *Cloth $4.95*